CONTEMPORARY
BRITISH
& IRISH
FICTION

AN INTRODUCTION
THROUGH INTERVIEWS

Sharon Monteith
University of Nottingham

Jenny Newman
Liverpool John Moores
University

Pat Wheeler
University of Hertfordshire

A member of the Hodder Headline Group
London
Distributed in the United States of America
by Oxford University Press Inc., New York

ARNOLD

First published in Great Britain in 2004 by
Arnold, a member of the Hodder Headline Group,
338 Euston Road, London NW1 3BH

http://www.arnoldpublishers.com

Distributed in the United States of America by
Oxford University Press Inc.,
198 Madison Avenue, New York, NY10016

British Library Cataloguing in Publication Data
A catalogue record for this book is available from the British Library

Library of Congress Cataloging-in-Publication Data
A catalog record for this book is available from the Library of Congress

ISBN 0 340 76087 7

1 2 3 4 5 6 7 8 9 10

Typeset in 10/14 pt Meridien Roman by
Phoenix Photosetting, Chatham, Kent

Printed and bound in Great Britain by The Bath Press Ltd

What do you think about this book? Or any other Arnold title?
Please send your comments to feedback.arnold@hodder.co.uk

For the writers who have freely and generously given
their time in interviews

Contents

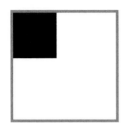

About the authors

Sharon Monteith is Reader in American Studies at the University of Nottingham. She publishes on American and British fiction and film. Her books include *Advancing Sisterhood? Interracial Friendships in Contemporary Southern Fiction* (University of Georgia Press, 2000); *Pat Barker* (Northcote House, 2002); *Gender and the Civil Rights Movement* (ed. with Peter Ling, 1999), *South to a New Place: Region, Literature, Culture* (ed. with Suzanne Jones, 2002), and *Critical Perspectives on Pat Barker* (ed. with Margaretta Jolly, Nahem Yousaf and Ronald Paul, University of South Carolina Press, forthcoming).

Jenny Newman is Reader in Creative Writing at Liverpool John Moores University. Her novels are *Going In* (Hamish Hamilton, 1994) and *Life Class* (Chatto & Windus, 1999), and her short fiction has appeared in *This Is*, *Pool* and *The London Magazine*. She is the editor of *The Faber Book of Seductions* (1988), and co-editor of *Women Talk Sex: Autobiographical Writing on Sex, Sexuality and Sexual Identity* (Scarlet Press, 1992) and *The Writer's Workbook* (Arnold, 2004).

Pat Wheeler is Senior Lecturer in Literature at the University of Hertfordshire. She publishes on British fiction, science fiction and contemporary women's writing. Her articles have appeared in *Critical Survey* and *Foundation*. She is a contributor to *Critical Perspectives on Pat Barker*, editor of *Critical Survey*, 'Imaginary Places: Representations of Dystopia in Literature and Film' (Autumn 2004) and the author of *Sebastian Faulks's Birdsong* (Continuum, 2002) and *Introduction to Science Fiction* (Continuum, forthcoming 2005).

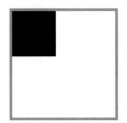

Acknowledgements

We would like to thank David Evans, James Friel and Nahem Yousaf for sharing their expertise by contributing to this volume and Jane Steele for transcribing the interviews.

Introduction: reading contemporary British and Irish fiction

Sharon Monteith, Jenny Newman and Pat Wheeler

State of the art

More people read fiction today than ever before. In spite of repetitive claims that the novel is dead, Britain and Ireland publish more novels per head of the population than almost any other country. The modern phenomena of readers' groups and television programmes such as *The Big Read* draw people's attention both to contemporary bestsellers and to classics. New titles fight weekly for our attention in huge chains of bookshops, supplements such as the *Guardian*'s recently launched *Review* assess authors old and new, and lucrative literary awards such as the Man Booker and Aer Lingus prizes continue to generate national and international publicity.

Nor has the novel been inched out by new media. British and Irish fiction is dramatised on television and radio, and adapted for our burgeoning film industry. Many writers interviewed in this volume discuss the gains and losses involved in adapting their novels for the screen, and Hanif Kureishi and Bernard Mac Laverty have both directed films. The internet offers an ever-expanding outlet, with hundreds of online magazines seeking fiction submissions, promoting their authors across the world, running competitions and spawning interactive hypertextuals. Many novelists now have their own websites, through which they promote recent work, publish their backlists, communicate with their readers or test new ideas in linked blogs. Kureishi often puts stories and essays on his website in advance of their publication in book form so that readers can see work in progress, and Fay Weldon began a novel in instalments on the Web.

When asked about the contemporary novel, the writers interviewed in this book identified a range of powerful voices writing in new kinds of English or new Englishes, and exploring what it means to be young, old, lesbian or gay, black British or disenfranchised, or to live at the heart of a vanishing empire.

But many writers also find cause for concern. Public funding for fiction is shrinking, and publishing houses, often owned by international agglomerates, are increasingly profit-oriented. The editor's role has dwindled, and few are allowed to foster their authors' careers through a period of modest sales. Nor would all writers agree with Hanif Kureishi, who believes that the work creates the market rather than the other way round. Marketing departments generate hype, and can come to dictate publishing strategy. Meanwhile, novelists seldom make a living, and independent bookshops close. The Net Book Agreement has been abolished, which means, as Michèle Roberts points out, that certain titles are promoted at the expense of others. Like many authors, she fears that we may not continue to cherish novels that are unfashionable, eccentric and without multiple selling points.

Though rich and diverse, contemporary British and Irish fiction is prey to assassin critics[1] (sometimes journalists who ravage fiction when they wish they could write it), who pronounce the British novel sickly and the risk of recovery slight, or dismiss the Irish novel as whimsical or stuck in a rut of Celtic nostalgia. Bemoaning the 'state' of the English novel has become a favourite national pastime. A. S. Byatt believes such attacks are just a 'journalistic commonplace' and defends the British novel and its immense variety from those who insist it is parochial and insular. She also cites a host of contemporary writers on this side of the Atlantic who she feels are as complex and interesting as their American counterparts.

If contemporary fiction is a barometer of the nation's intellectual health, then Britain and Ireland are very well indeed. Irvine Welsh and Bernard Mac Laverty, for instance, place themselves firmly within a Celtic tradition, and cite the work of James Joyce, Flann O'Brien and Lewis Grassic Gibbon, with Mac Laverty quoting scenes and images that infuse his own aesthetics; but he and Welsh also admire more recent writers such as William McIlvanney, James Kelman and Brian Moore. The Irish Roddy Doyle finds he is as likely to be influenced by the very English Dickens or the American Upton Sinclair as Flann O'Brien. Feeling a lack of a women's working-class tradition when she began to write, Pat Barker turned to African American writers for the techniques of transforming the individual voice into a communal one.

This volume takes seismographs of the contemporary literary landscape. All the writers interviewed are favourites with the reading public; and some, like Unsworth and Weldon, have staked out their literary terrain over the last four decades or more. Some – Barker, Doyle and Unsworth – are Booker Prize winners; others would seem to write *not* to be shortlisted. When Angela Carter reviewed Kureishi's *The Buddha of Suburbia*, she singled it out as 'the first novel in what I trust will be a rapidly growing and influential genre, the novel designed on purpose to exclude itself from the Booker short list'.[2] Welsh even goes so far as to state that he is 'the sort of writer who should be detested by critics. I wouldn't be doing my job if I was praised.'

However, none of the writers we interviewed has remained a fixed exemplar. Hollinghurst believes his style changes with each new book. Reviewers maintained that Pat Barker changed direction with the start of her First World War trilogy. The setting for Doyle's Barrytown trilogy may be geographically close to that of *A Star Called Henry* but these novels are worlds apart in style and form. Weldon and Kureishi shift gears with the signs of the times, Weldon even writing a 'product placement' novel. Welsh signals difference in another way: he is a writer for whom English literature is 'tied to culturally elitist baggage' and so combines his sardonic explorations of Edinburgh's underclass with strong views on the Scottish novel, arguing that if you put a group of English writers together in a bar you would get 'a pretty fair representation of Oxbridge'; whereas you could put a group of Scottish novelists in a bar and they'd be, 'socially speaking, a pretty fair representation of Scottish people'. Open and perceptive in their interviews, the writers here hail the novel's variety, the plurality of its voices and forms – and the debates it generates.

History and memory

From Barry Unsworth's classical Greece to Fay Weldon's 1960s, history is a lens through which we scrutinise the present. A. S. Byatt – to her surprise – sees herself as a historical novelist and Unsworth declares that 'the uses to which the past has been put is arguably the single most important development of the last quarter of a century'. The critic Franco Moretti argues that the images and forms we use to picture historical moments are 'crucial for the fashioning of our identity'.[3] In the British and Irish context, the colonial past is traced in myriad ways. George Eliot famously observed, 'there is no private life which has not been determined by a wider public life'. In *A Star Called Henry*, Doyle's Henry Star is born in 1901, stands in the Dublin post office at the start of the Easter Rising, and becomes a rebel fighter under Michael Collins. Like Barker's Liza born in 1900 in *Liza's England*, or Rushdie's Saleem Sinai born as the clock strikes 12 in 1947 to signal the Partition of India in *Midnight's Children*, the central character living-in-history helps the reader to imagine alternative pasts, and to challenge those imposed through 'national narratives' or 'official history'. As Hayden

White observes, 'The historical past is, in a word, "uncanny," both known and unknown, present and absent, familiar and alien, at one and the same time. Thus construed, the historical past has all the attributes that we might ascribe to the psychological sphere of the "imaginary".'[4] Barker shows that the ways in which we remember do not exist in a social vacuum. In *Another World* the 101-year-old veteran's memory of the First World War is dictated by society and modified as ideological fashions change. Fiction which draws on the past is essentially paradoxical, simultaneously representing and resisting history. In Irish novels from William Trevor's *Fools of Fortune* to Patrick McCabe's *The Dead School*, memory is often cathartic but rarely restorative. Writers including Edna O'Brien, John Banville, Roddy Doyle, Dermot Healy and Jamie O'Neil examine Ireland through painfully emotional evocations of history and a sense of place. In Seamus Deane's *Reading in the Dark* each memory becomes a layer in a palimpsest conveying the narrator's turmoil over the shadowy presence of his Republican gunman uncle.

Many novels shift between different eras, such as Roberts's *In the Red Kitchen* and *The Mistressclass*, Unsworth's *Stone Virgin*, Barker's *Liza's England* and *Another World*, and Byatt's *Possession*. The powerful force of memory often presented in first-person narrative reveals that time is vertiginous for some (Barker's Geordie and Roberts's Hattie). Barker has discussed the importance of wearing one's research lightly; to overload the novel with extraneous detail is to overwhelm the story. Roberts agrees, feeling that for a writer who undertakes research, everything is linked to everything else in a crystalline way: 'that's what's underneath every novel, the world of the unconscious, which is a library as well. The reading doesn't necessarily show, but it's there and you keep going back to it.' For Doyle, as for many other writers, character always comes first and 'history follows along afterwards'. Barry Unsworth says 'it is astonishing how little one needs to write about the past in order to convince the reader that it's an authentic picture. There's a common illusion that you have to pile detail on detail.' Weldon goes even further: 'if you need to research a particular topic then you'd better not write the novel in question'. She is convinced that writing is 'something you know about innately'. For Unsworth the historical novel is never 'just a question of historical research but historical imagination'.

When writers turn to the recent past they may uncover the ways in which living memory is subject to nostalgia and painful recall. *The Anatomy School*, for instance, looks back to the beginning of the 1960s, a turbulent time both in Ireland and in the wider world. Mac Laverty is aware of how the decade affects his creativity: 'I was twenty-seven in 1969, and around me there was anarchy, murder and mayhem. You want to deal with that in writing.' For Roberts and Weldon especially, the 1960s was the decade in which women became their own historical subject, 'looking back through their mothers', to borrow Virginia Woolf's axiom, and drew inspiration from the Women's Liberation Movement in rediscovering a female literary tradition. Weldon's *Down Among the Women* became an iconic feminist text, and Byzantia a youthful role model. Weldon remembers writing it 'because I couldn't find the book I wanted to read about the dire predicament of women', although she refuses to glorify the decade.

Lesbian writers also tested their theories in novels such May Sarton's *A Reckoning* and Roberts's *A Piece of the Night*. Jeanette Winterson's coming-out story, *Oranges Are Not the Only Fruit*, combined humour with a sharp sense of the 1960s in the North of England, and drew in even the most homophobic reader when published in 1985. As Kureishi says in his interview for this book, during the Thatcher years it seemed important to write about transgressive desire.

Writing Britain and Ireland

In the 1980s Margaret Thatcher declared that there was no such thing as society; Britain had lost its place on the world stage, yet the government led the country into armed conflict in the Falklands and into the (first) Gulf War. Racial and urban violence at home led poet Linton Kwesi Johnson to the conclusion that 'Inglan is a bitch / There's no escapin' it'. The welfare state was being dismantled and the 1982 Nationality Act conferred British citizenship on some whilst denying it to others who had made Britain their home for decades. In June 1988 Clause 28 of the Local Government Act ricocheted around Parliament, the result of a debate on books for children such as *Jenny Lives with Eric and Martin*. It became illegal for local authorities to 'intentionally promote homosexuality', a phrase that would lead to continuous debate until the clause was repealed in Scotland in 2000 and in the rest of the United Kingdom in March 2003. Alan Hollinghurst says that ironically the clause helped to promote *The Swimming-Pool Library*: 'it was held up as the sort of thing that might be banned from public libraries'. Paul Magrs's recent novel *Strange Boy* has caught the tail end of that debate. His story of a 10-year-old boy's discovery that he is gay, though condemned by certain Christian and teachers' groups, has received backing from the Chartered Institute of Library and Information Professionals. As the decade opened in Ireland, unemployment was around 20 per cent and rising to the second highest in the 'developed' world; the national debt was dangerously high and would not be turned around until the 1990s. PAYE marches and high emigration figures for those *leaving* Ireland swelled the sense of crisis in the early 1980s. In the North, the Maze prison hit the headlines when Republican prisoners launched a hunger strike in which 10 men died, and the Troubles dominated the news.

Postmodernist ideas of a decentred subject seemed to deny political agency to individuals and groups who were just finding their voices in politics as well as fiction. In Livi Michael's *Under a Thin Moon* young women protagonists eke out a living on a Manchester council estate and fantasise about escape. Their author's fractured, postmodernist style embodies their failure to connect in any significant way in 1980s Britain. Black British writing in the 1980s began charting – in novels such as Joan Riley's *Waiting in the Twilight* – the depressing experiences of African Caribbean families and the ongoing discrimination they faced. These were unhappy fictions describing what black British novelist Barbara Burford once called 'a little black pain undressed'.

Nevertheless, the best writing often came from oppressed or marginalised figures. Burford set her 1986 novella *The Threshing Floor* in Canterbury, that most English of towns, where Chaucer's pilgrims ended their journey. She confidently creates black British characters whose presence is as established in this small, academic and largely rural community as in the inner cities. *My Beautiful Laundrette*, Kureishi's first screenplay, also published in 1986, turned Thatcherite business acumen into bristling comedy drama in which a young Asian man and a fascist member of the National Front fall in love as they turn a run-down launderette into a going concern. The rites of passage novel inevitably builds on a strong sense of place and evocation of a particular decade. In Iain Banks's *The Crow Road* a young man comes of age in the 1980s in the North of Scotland. Prentice's reality is conveyed through the mass media – what was in the news, in the charts and on the television – in a postmodernist family saga as accessible as a soap opera. Writers like Banks, Kureishi and Burford renegotiated aspects of 'Britishness', recognising its inherent hybridity, and indeed its slipperiness in a difficult decade.

Norman Tebbit's infamous 'cricket test' of 1990 forms one of the epigraphs to Zadie Smith's *White Teeth*, but rather than attempting to answer the question about which team black Britons cheer for, 'looking back to where you came from or where you are', Smith gives the lie to Tebbit's right-wing fantasy of immigration as an inevitable 'clash of history . . . of religion . . . of race . . . of violence'. She explores the complexities of cross-cultural relationships, forged in and after the Second World War and played out in London. Irvine Welsh's *Maribou Stork Nightmares* opens with Prime Minister John Major's statement of 1993 that in Britain 'we should condemn [a little] more and understand [a little] less'. Welsh unpacks Major's aphorism through the character of soccer hooligan Roy Strang, who participates in a gang rape but who as a child suffered brutality and abuse. A number of writers choose to address ethical dilemmas: Barker in *Border Crossing* and *Double Vision* through the possible rehabilitation of the child murderer, Danny Miller, which proved uncannily prescient when the killers of James Bulger were released from prison. Edna O'Brien tackles a different ethical quandary in *Down By the River* and Roddy Doyle's rendition of the alcoholic wife Paula Spencer in *The Woman Who Walked Into Doors* is a clear-sighted exegesis of the emotional effects of domestic abuse.

The collapse of romantic relationships and marriages is common in contemporary fiction, as in Ian McEwan's *The Comfort of Strangers*, *The Child in Time* and *Enduring Love*. Beleaguered males have begun to feature in fiction by younger writers: Nick Hornby comes closest to the autobiographical when he explores the position of a middle-aged father living apart from his child in *31 Songs*. Male anti-heroes are not an innovation in themselves – characters such as Patrick Standish and Roger Micheldene in Kingsley Amis's *Take A Girl Like You* and *One Fat Englishman* exuded a kind of disturbing charm in the 1960s – but they are a factor of contemporary life that Kureishi made his own in *Intimacy* and in a number of short stories where middle-aged protagonists reach a point of crisis and break away from former lives and loves with 'family' the casualty. Kureishi has here tapped into a contemporary anxiety and, as he notes in his interview, possibly a new readership.

Roots and regions

In his introduction to *The Penguin Book of Irish Fiction*, novelist Colm Toibin deliberates on the relationship of Irish writers to their homeland. Irish literature, he says, 'is distinguished by its passionate voice and by its keen awareness of Ireland's political troubles, especially regarding England'. The purpose of much Irish fiction, he believes, is to 'become involved in the Irish argument', and the purpose of much Irish criticism, in turn, 'has been to relate the fiction to the argument'.[5] John Banville, the award-winning writer of *The Book of Evidence*, states:

The relationship between England and Ireland is still very strange, and it's not just bombs and bullets. Geographically, it's strange in that Ireland is a post-colonial nation with the former colonists living only seventy miles across the sea. If they were halfway around the world, I'm sure we wouldn't be as obsessed with the English as we are.[6]

Banville's *The Untouchable* is a commentary on this precise aspect of the British–Irish relationship, although he is quick to point out that obsessions with the political past may not be shared by younger writers. He might almost have been thinking of Anna Burns's debut novel, *No Bones*, which explores the effects of violence from a woman's perspective. The novel opens in 1969, when British troops were sent to Belfast, and ends in 1994, the year of the IRA ceasefire, but Burns also tries to imagine a future in which conflict is absent.

English novelist Will Self visited the province in 1994 and interviewed young writers Robert McLiam Wilson, Glenn Patterson and Carlo Gebler. He described them as 'narrative artisans' because, in his view, Northern Irish writers have 'had to fabricate their own stories with a will, because the story the society was telling itself was so warped'.[7] Political fiction plays a central literary role in Northern Ireland. In this volume, Bernard Mac Laverty explains that he finds it impossible to avoid the Troubles and most specifically the religious and class segregation that coloured his early life. Even *Grace Notes*, set on Islay and in Glasgow, opens with Catherine McKenna's journey back to the pub where she grew up on the edge of Belfast.

Yet the Irish novel has escaped a rigid sense of discretely Protestant and Catholic writing traditions, or Southern versus Northern distinctions resting on dour images of Protestants and fanatical IRA gunmen, or romantic Catholic gaels and rural eccentrics. Instead, it offers a range of fictional representations, as in Colin Bateman's *Wild About Harry*, *Mohammed Maguire*, *Turbulent Priests* and the darkly comic *Reservoir Pups* and *Chapter and Verse*; or as in new writing by women: Nicola Lindsay's *Eden Fading*, Erin Kaye's *Mothers and Daughters*, Martina Devlin's *Venus Reborn* and Kate O'Riordan's *Involved*.

The 1980s was a watershed in Scottish literature, and Scottish identities were 'remade' by writers such as Alasdair Gray (*Lanark*), James Kelman (*The Busconductor Hines*), Janice Galloway (*The Trick is to Keep Breathing*) and Alan Warner (*The Sopranos*, *Morvern Callar*, *These Demented Lands*). Gray's *Lanark: A Life in 4 Books*, a political allegory cast in the tradition of science fiction, is perhaps most representative of that watershed, while Kelman's *The Busconductor Hines* and *How Late it Was, How Late* have influenced a new generation of Scottish writers. The Welsh novel is undergoing a revival with crime fiction by novelists such as Bill James (*Split* and *A Man's Enemies*), whose books often feature Simon Abelard, a black graduate recruited by British Intelligence as a spy on returning to Cardiff; Anna Davies's *Melting Pot*, about the criminal art of conning people; and Sean Burke's *Deadwater*, based on the gruesome and infamous murder of prostitute Lynette White, for which the 'Cardiff Three' were imprisoned and later released after wrongful conviction was proved. In *Un Nos Ola Leuad* (*One Moonlit Night*), Caradog Pritchard grapples with taboos including insanity and incest and religious excesses. Niall Griffiths's *Grits* focuses on a community of drug addicts and alcoholics in Aberystwyth and has been dubbed the Welsh equivalent of *Trainspotting*.

'Welsh noir' involves the struggles of a nonconformist culture as a new nation attempts to find its place in British society. Wales has also seen a rich mix of debut novels in recent years by John Williams, Trezza Azzopardi, Peter Ho Davies and Niall Griffiths. As in Scotland, the devolution debates and tensions between England and the Welsh nationalists have become a thematic concern. In *Sheepshagger* Griffiths explores tensions between the Welsh and English owners of 'holiday homes', and in 'The Ugliest House in the World', the title story from his prize-winning collection, Peter Ho Davies, of mixed Chinese and Welsh heritage himself, tackles the cultural contradictions inherent in an elderly Welshman's return 'home' after some 40 years of family life in England. The rural Wales Davies describes is very different from Cardiff's multicultural Tiger Bay, or Merthyr Tydfil, the setting for Desmond Barry's *A Bloody Good Friday*. Like Zadie Smith in *The Autograph Man*, Davies exhibits the freedom to write across cultural lines by imagining a Jewish protagonist in *The Bad Shepherd*. Trezza Azzopardi's debut novel, *The Hiding Place*, shortlisted for the Booker Prize, chronicles the life of a Maltese immigrant family in 1960s Cardiff, drawing on childhood memories of family violence and poverty, and a community that would otherwise be invisible in contemporary fiction.

As D. J. Taylor has noted, one is now as likely to find British fiction telling a story of Huddersfield or Birmingham or Glasgow or Cornwall as London.[8] The 'provincial' backlash can be glossed as a reaction against Thatcherite centrism in the 1980s. Yet the British novel has always been provincial – with the odd glance at London. Who could be seen as more 'English' than the Brontës, Thomas Hardy, Elizabeth Gaskell or George Eliot? Byatt believes that Arnold Bennett and D. H. Lawrence were far better writers than the 'Wains and the Braines', as she calls them, could ever hope to be. Also, the London novel is itself fissured. Women writers in the 1970s spoke resonantly about the metropolis. Early novels by Roberts and Weldon were set in Islington. Angela Carter was defiantly a South London novelist. Timothy Mo's *Sour Sweet* presents a differently viewed multicultural South London in which white Londoners in the 1960s are the 'pink-faced foreign' customers who all look the same to his Chinese restaurateurs. Zadie Smith's Willesden, Byatt's Putney, Monica Ali's Brick Lane and Philip Hensher's Parliament seem to be different towns. The point is brought even more forcibly home in fiction about another diverse city: Doyle's Henry Smart discovers in *A Star Called Henry* that New York at the beginning of the twentieth century is 'a collection of European villages'; but in Rushdie's *Fury*, set a century later, we see instead a high-tech globalisation, consumerism and fashion: a postmodern anywhere and everywhere. Myths of 'Englishness' help shape an image of the nation that is satirised with comic brio by writers such as Gordon Burn and Hanif Kureishi. But the mythology can repel when presented as a paragon of excellence. In *Lucy*, Jamaica Kincaid's schoolgirl protagonist is obliged to memorise Wordsworth's 'Daffodils' while at Queen Victoria Girls' School in Antigua. When she finally sees a field of the real flowers, she wishes for an enormous scythe to mow down the 'beautiful' motif of Britain's cultural imperialism. Kincaid's imagery is a potent reminder of a fact of British life that E. R. Braithewaite summarised in *To Sir With Love*: that it is 'wonderful' for the former colonised to be British – until they come to Britain.

Good fiction has always challenged the establishment. Thomas Hardy was censored and, as a result, stopped writing fiction decades before he died. The Brontë sisters were widely thought scandalous – yet now they are in the top 21 of the nation's polls for *The Big Read*, sitting oddly alongside the Harry Potter books which, although they have charmed readers around the world, have also been banned in some parts of America for supposedly anti-Christian content. Lawrence and Joyce were both censored and Clause 28 persuaded some educators and librarians to exercise choice for young readers based on little more than a moral panic. Edna O'Brien was dismayed when her brave and frank picture of young women in *The Country Girls* was described as a 'smear on Irish womanhood' and banned in Ireland. Michèle Roberts in a 1986 essay, 'Write, She Said', explores what might be the serio-comic repercussions of writing a 'lesbian sado-masochistic romantic pornographic epic' when one's writerly self is split by self-expectation and self-censorship: 'whether your readers will see what you produce as a romance is another matter'.[9] Roddy Doyle was criticised for his portrayal of domestic violence in the series he wrote for television, *The Family*, but fights back: 'I'm not a branch of the tourist industry and I don't see it as my job to present an idealistic version of Ireland, or Irish families.'

The world elsewhere

William Trevor left County Cork in the 1950s and has often said that to write about Ireland he needs to remain at a geographical distance from it. Edna O'Brien, Brian Moore and Deirdre Madden feel the same. In *August is a Wicked Month*, O'Brien's Ellen, holidaying in France, denies she even comes from Ireland because people immediately start talking about 'fairies and grandmothers'; but the distance does allow her to think more clearly of what 'home' may mean to her. Bernard Mac Laverty left Belfast for Scotland as a young man and lends equal weight to both locations in his novels and stories. Conversely, Hilary Mantel, a British-born writer of Irish heritage, has always written about Ireland from a distance and believes she may have invented a language in which to do so – an 'English moved sideways' as she calls it.[10] In 'No Passport Required', an essay in which she takes up the idea of Benedict Anderson's imagined communities, she recalls how she began to define herself as a 'European writer' who is more at 'home' in Ireland and in Europe though born into post-war England. Her dismissal of the terms 'British writer' and 'English writer' combines the stuff of intellectual debate with the intensely personal: 'To me, the first description is meaningless. "Britain" can be used as a geographical term, but it has no definable cultural meaning. As for calling me "an English writer" – it is simply what I am not.' The co-ordinates of her discussion are the axioms – descent, religion, region, accent – and the exclusionary terms – provincial and Anglocentric – that continue to dominate many literary conversations about region and nation. Mantel believes 'it is the role of writers and artists to make sure that the idea of a nation is not regressive, not repressive'.[11] For others such as Roddy Doyle and Glen Patterson in Ireland, Kureishi in London or Barker in the North East of England, it is staying put that continually charges their fictional themes and settings, although Doyle wonders whether in his more recent work – lighting out for New York and Chicago – he is following those Irish who left the country in the 1920s and headed West.

In 2003 Ian Jack noted that British novelists 'like abroad'.[12] Its lure has long been a theme for both British and Irish writers, island people fascinated by travel. Going abroad is not a new direction when one considers Kipling's life in India, Lawrence's wanderings in Australia and Mexico, or Orwell's in France, Spain and Burma. Even P. G. Wodehouse, doyen of English gentlemen, spent long periods 'elsewhere'. British and Irish writers often take their novels to the European mainland – for entertainment or moments of revelation. For many modern writers, 'abroad' remains the end of a quest (Patricia Duncker's *Hallucinating Foucault*; Unsworth's *Losing Nelson*); the site of a revelation or tragedy (Barker's *Double Vision*; Roberts's *The Mistressclass*). As writers move around, they strike out against insularity – 'what should they know of England who only England know?' – and extend the novel's range and scope. Many have taken on America: Kureishi's *The Buddha of Suburbia*, Martin Amis's *Money* and Zadie Smith's *The Autograph Man* all have protagonists who go to New York for at least a third of the book. In Peter Preston's novel *51st State* Britain has become little more than an American outpost by 2022. In Roddy Doyle's *The Commitments* the young Dubliners co-opt the Motown sound to create their own 'Dublin soul' and in Patrick Neate's *Twelve Bar Blues* New Orleans jazz and the Louisiana bayou are the initial inspiration for a narrative that spans two centuries and crosses three continents.

In 1988 Terry Eagleton asserted that the importation of literary 'outsiders' or visitors with their 'exotic' perspectives would revive British fiction.[13] Oddly, he failed to note the solid body of fiction already written by Britons themselves, insiders though often considered outsiders, such as Kazuo Ishiguro, Caryl Phillips, Timothy Mo and Salman Rushdie, whose work is rooted in British cultural conditions. Some of the most incisive depictions of contemporary Britain and Ireland come from those who bring to their descriptions an experience of elsewhere – of life outside Britain or of hearing ancestral stories from other parts of the world. In the very year that Eagleton was writing, Rushdie published *The Satanic Verses*, a novel in which Indian immigrants fall out of the sky and land on an English beach.

Caryl Phillips and Fred D'Aguiar have written black people back into the British landscape. Barry Unsworth and Caryl Phillips explore the nation's colonies and ex-colonies. Kureishi, like an insider with outsider information, helps transform the ideological space that the British novel encompasses. Where George Orwell once talked about the hole in the centre of English writing as the space in which working-class lives should be described and imagined, Hanif Kureishi drew readers' attention to a hole in the centre of contemporary British writing, a gap and a silence about the lives of black Britons. Kureishi noted this omission in the early 1980s and the gap is closing, filling up with writers and novels since his superbly comic *The Buddha of Suburbia* in which an 'Englishman born and bred, well almost' negotiates a place for his dreams and aspirations in suburban England in the 1970s. The British novel has become an international phenomenon: it draws on British characters with histories that encompass India, Africa and the Caribbean especially, and it confronts Britain's legacies of slavery and colonialism in particular, in Unsworth's *Sacred Hunger*, Kureishi's *The Black Album* and Monica Ali's *Brick Lane*, novels in which the dispossessed become possessed of their own history.

Anglo-French connections are pursued creatively by novelists as different from each other as John Berger, Michèle Roberts and Julian Barnes. Ian McEwan has set novels in Berlin as well as in Britain, and Pauline Melville has written about Guyana. Patricia Duncker takes *James Miranda Barry* to the Caribbean. Weldon, Unsworth, Byatt, Mac Laverty, Hollinghurst and Barker have all at points in their literary careers chosen to write about remote rural settings, though Roberts and Unsworth have gone to Europe in order to do so. Many writers have homes in continental Europe – Muriel Spark, Barry Unsworth, Lisa St Aubin de Teran – or seem to have dual nationality, like Marina Warner and Michèle Roberts. In other words, it could be said that expatriate life in France or Italy has become a new sort of province in British and Irish fiction. Barker alludes to a professional traveller, V. S. Naipual, whose *Enigma of Arrival* she admires for what it reveals about seeing the nation through 'foreign eyes': when Naipaul sets off around Britain, far from defamiliarising the places he visits, he discovers the nation absorbs him. The idea returns us to Orwell in *The English People* and to his essay 'The Lion and the Unicorn', in which he talks of England having 'the power to change out of recognition, and yet remain the same'.

Literary architecture

Each of the writers we interview comments in some way on the architecture of fiction: plots and structuring, narrative strategies and processes. Alan Hollinghurst is surprised at how personal his work is: 'My writing is deeply about me, often in ways I don't see until a long time afterwards, and even though I have never written in any way autobiographically.' Barker and Welsh, Roberts and Kureishi each return to their families when articulating the past. As Roberts says, 'parents stand in for all the people in history whom I've never met but want to know', and Kureishi maintains that his father was his major influence. Welsh and Mac Laverty come from families of storytellers and Barker remembers the voices of her great aunts, 'quarrelling about what happened on a particular day in 1911 because the past still mattered passionately'.

Writers like to turn language inside out, to flex words as they flex ideas. Barker talks in detail about the way that 'dialogue in books seems like normal speech but is actually a very special sort of language'. There is no easy critical vocabulary in which to talk about dialogue but she finds metaphors with which to approach it (as 'sculpted silence') and terms through which to examine it ('apparently unselfconscious' and 'hyperconscious' dialogue). For a number of the writers interviewed, dialect is important to a novel's rhythm: Roddy Doyle, Irvine Welsh and Bernard Mac Laverty each discuss ways to hear as well as read the spoken voice as dialect. Doyle distinguishes carefully between his refusal to gloss the Dublin demotic in the Barrytown trilogy and the importance of translating the Irish language in *Paddy Clarke Ha Ha Ha*. Claiming that readers are accustomed to 'standard English', critics have often found novels in dialect a problem and many see inherent difficulties in reading phonetic transcription. However, recent fiction has started to combat the suppression of dialect. Doyle and Welsh go out of their way to use vernacular rhythms and expressions. William McIlvanney sees that 'Scots words love to dismantle attitudes' and that as a Scottish writer all he can do is 'inhabit the paradoxes as healthily as possible and try to embrace the dichotomies' that occur when one language is suppressed at the expense of another.[14] Language and vocabulary are an effective way to disrupt standard narratives and narrate 'missing' voices. Doyle emphasises the creativity of slang and the importance of capturing the way Dublin people really talk.

As B. S. Johnson discerned in *Aren't You Rather Young to be Writing Your Memoirs*, 'Life does not tell stories. Life is chaotic, fluid, random; it leaves myriads of ends untied, untidily. Writers can extract a story from life only by strict, close selection, and this must mean falsification. Telling stories is really telling lies.'[15] For Welsh the 'basic building blocks' of a good novel are a good story, strong characters and honesty. Byatt, like Unsworth and Mac Laverty, feels that she owes her readers a story; and Alan Hollinghurst feels 'the wonderful thing about fiction' is 'you read about all sorts of experiences that are not your own'. But building the story to its best effects and struggling with the literary problems that arise is the key challenge: for Michèle Roberts it involves the quest to find a beautiful shape for novels and for Barry Unsworth the technical challenge is always linked to the author's self-discovery. The metaphors of building and restoring are themselves made intrinsic to the novel-making process, in *Sacred Hunger* through the building of the slave ship, and in *Stone Virgin* the restoration of Girolamo's statue relates to the solving of a mystery, and, more importantly, builds self-recognition on the part of the restorer.

Following James Joyce and B. S. Johnson, some contemporary writers continue to experiment with the consciously avant-garde – notably Jonathan Coe in *The Rotters' Club*, James Kelman in *Translated Accounts* and Eva Figes in *The Knot*. Experiments with typography alter the texture of the novel, as in *Maribou Stork Nightmares*, where Welsh uses different orthographies to signal the moments when Roy Strang's story switches between three different temporal and geographical spaces, or Zadie Smith's *The Autograph Man*, which includes diagrams and pop quizzes, and stories boxed off in the speech bubbles reminiscent of comic books.

Sometimes what once appeared experimental has become folded into a typology of narrative techniques, as in the case of the 'unreliable narrator', a term and technique that the critic Wayne C. Booth first discussed in detail in his 1961 *The Rhetoric of Fiction*. A worm narrates part of Welsh's *Filth*, and Roddy Doyle's 10-year-old Paddy Clarke in the eponymous Booker Prize-winning novel spins a web of lies – in B. S. Johnson's sense, perhaps. Unreliable narrators are favoured by Irvine Welsh, who says that the old dichotomies between fantasy and realism don't exist any more: 'if you fantasise, it's real'. In the historiographical novel 'traditional' markers of history – figures, events, periodisation – can be the stuff of catechresis, puzzling rather than elucidatory. In Graham Swift's *Waterland*, for example, history is a 'cumbersome but precious bag of clues' that Swift scatters liberally throughout a text that refuses to settle comfortably into a single generic category.

Pat Barker's first three novels uncompromisingly explored and exposed the 'condition of England' in the North East, focusing on women's experiences of the deindustrialisation of working-class communities, and Doyle's Barrytown trilogy performed a similar role for Dublin. However, contemporary realist and naturalist novelists are erroneously deemed to stand outside aesthetic concerns, as if their fictions function as mere windows on the world. The same blinkered attitude assumes that postmodernist fictional practices are synonymous with complexity and anarchic thought, and that those writers who draw on realist techniques oppose the dominance of postmodernist ideas in contemporary fiction. Yet few of the writers interviewed see themselves as postmodernists. A. S. Byatt, for instance, describes herself as a realist writer – albeit a self-conscious one – and feels that novelists still have not learned from the technical innovations introduced by E. M. Forster and D. H. Lawrence. Barry Unsworth does not like clashes of discourse, and prefers not to let what he calls the 'ragged edges' show. For a sense of tradition he looks back to Eudora Welty, and defines himself as belonging to the 'tail-end of the realist–modernist movement'.

Almost all the writers in this collection jibbed at our question about the usefulness of critical labels: 'you walk away from a label as fast as you can', in Barker's view. Even generic labels produced a wave of distrust. Both Pat Barker and Roddy Doyle objected to the term 'novel of ideas', especially for character-driven novels; while in his most recent work, Rushdie makes a historian of ideas a cult figure and his main protagonist. Alan Hollinghurst understands that he may be labelled a 'gay writer' but hopes that the term will not obscure other important facets of his fiction; Irvine Welsh and Pat Barker are equally wearied by the simplistic assumption that if the writer comes from a working-class background the novels are assumed to be autobiographical in nature.

In her witty, affectionate satire of the academics in *Possession*, A. S. Byatt proves herself an expert on critical theory. She is, however, hostile to its destruction of the pleasure principle, and its abolition of the author's role. Michèle Roberts believes that critical theory can help you read more richly, but loathes the kind of theory which appears to obliterate works of art. Few of the authors interviewed here discuss their work in theoretical terms, unless to focus on the role of the unconscious. Fay Weldon describes the process of writing first drafts as 'a sleep walk'. Roberts sees the unconscious as part of the writer herself, sending her messages if she tunes in and does her work. Most of these writers could be seen as pragmatists who focus on technique: Barker discusses her use of dialogue, and how to structure a novel with timeshifts; Mac Laverty speaks of the importance of titles. Hanif Kureishi says that he looks for his characters' 'moment of crisis', when some substantial component in their life is breaking down, and begins writing there because that moment is so dramatic. Roberts, too, talks about how each novel represents a problem to be solved, demanding the invention of a new form. Unsworth goes back one stage further, seeing young writers wasting time by starting on novels they are not equipped for, simply because they believe they are producing the right kind of book for its time. It is more to the point, he says, to find a voice that corresponds with one's abilities. Even the acquisition of technique matters less, he feels, than finding out what kind of writer one is.

These interviews deal mostly with the writing process rather than the product, discussing problems which may have since been resolved in finished novels. The writer Charles Foran points out that works in progress are always precarious;[16] or, as Michèle Roberts puts it, frightening 'because it's about getting lost. It's a serious madness, it really is; you feel you've somehow disintegrated and will never come back.' At the end of his interview Hanif Kureishi says how important it is not to see your latest novel as the last word in the process: 'You write in light and dark.'

Notes

1 See Malcolm Bradbury, 'To Tell the Truth about Fiction', *Sunday Times* (10 Jan. 1994), pp. 10–11. He discusses 'assassin critics' in *The Modern British Novel* (Harmondsworth: Penguin, 1993).

2 Angela Carter, 'A Candide in Bromley' quoted in Nahem Yousaf, *Hanif Kureishi's The Buddha of Suburbia* (London: Continuum, 2002), p. 58.

3 Franco Moretti, 'The Spell of Indecision', in Cary Nelson and Lawrence Grossberg, eds, *Marxism and the Interpretation of Culture* (London: Macmillan, 1988), p. 341.

4 Hayden White, *The Content of Form: Narrative Discourse and Historical Representation* (Baltimore: Johns Hopkins University Press, 1987), p. 37.

5 Colm Toibin, 'Introduction', *The Penguin Book of Irish Fiction* (Harmondsworth: Penguin, 2000).

6 Ron Hogan, 'Interview with John Banville', at www.beatrice.com/interviews/banville/

7 Will Self, 'A Little Cottage Industry', *Observer* (10 July 1994), pp. 20, 22, 24, 26.

8 D. J. Taylor, 'The New Literary Map of Britain', *The Sunday Times* (8 May 1994).

9 Michèle Roberts, 'Write, She Said', in Jean Radford, ed., *The Progress of Romance: The Politics of Popular Fiction* (London: Routledge, Kegan & Paul, 1986), p. 234.

10 Fernando Galvan, 'On Ireland, Religion and History: A Conversation with Hilary Mantel', *The European English Messenger* 10: 2 (Autumn 2001), p. 35.

11 Hilary Mantel, 'No Passport Required', *Guardian Review* (12 Oct. 2002), pp. 5–7. An extended version of Mantel's essay is published in Zachary Leader, ed., *On Modern British Fiction* (Oxford: Oxford University Press, 2002).

12 Ian Jack, preface to *Granta 81: Best of Young British Novelists 2003* (London: Granta, 2003), p. 12.

13 Terry Eagleton, *New Left Review* 172 (Nov.–Dec. 1988).

14 See Isabel Murray, 'Plato in a Boiler Suit: William McIlvanney', in Isobel Murray and Bob Tait, eds, *Scottish Writers Talking* (East Lothian: Tuckwell Press, 1996).

15 B. S. Johnson from the introduction to *Aren't You Rather Young to be Writing Your Memoirs*, repr. in Malcolm Bradbury, ed., *The Novel Today* (London: Fontana, 1977), pp. 151–68.

16 Charles Foran in Michael Ondaatje, Michael Redhill, Esta Spalding and Linda Spalding, eds, *Writers on Books Loved and Lost* (London: Bloomsbury, 2003), p. 59.

Pat Barker

Sharon Monteith

Pat Barker is the award-winning author of 10 novels and an occasional writer of short stories. She was awarded a CBE in 1999 and since she began publishing in 1982, when encouraged by Angela Carter to send her work to Virago, she has successfully captured the social and emotional landscape of contemporary Britain. Her first fictions are set in a post-industrial wasteland in the North of England and the pithy depiction of working-class lives in the 1970s and 1980s is unrelieved by a middle-class perspective or commentary, in order to explore how gender and class shape our understanding of labour and capitalism. She casts further back in time in *Liza's England* to examine the life of an octogenarian born in 1900 who, as she approaches the end of her life in 1984, begins telling her stories to a young social worker. Barker intervenes creatively in our collective and historical memories of the Second World War and small-town life in the 1950s (*The Man Who Wasn't There*) and of the First World War in the acclaimed *Regeneration* trilogy, in which she combines fictional characters including the effervescent Billy Prior with historical figures, notably the soldier-poets Siegfried Sassoon and Wilfred Owen and the army psychiatrist W. H. R. Rivers. Through her interest in issues of memory, sexuality, psychology, crime and random violence in the novels that follow – from *Another World* to *Double Vision* – she has tapped into the kinds of social anxieties that animate discussions of modern Britain.

Her first published novel, *Union Street*, was made into the film *Stanley and Iris* (directed by Martin Ritt) in 1990, but with Jane Fonda and Robert De Niro taking the leads it bears little resemblance to the source novel. In 1997 Gilles Mackinnon directed *Regeneration* (released in the USA as *Behind the Line*s). It is a disturbing anti-war film in its own right, though it elides the homoerotic tension that Barker implies between the shellshocked soldiers in order to focus on cross-generational relationships and literary friendships. Winner of the Booker Prize in 1995 and Author of the Year in 1996, and recipient of many other markers of esteem, including the Fawcett Prize for her debut novel, Barker continues to secure readers from school age to old age.

Key works

Union Street. London: Virago, 1982.

Blow Your House Down. London: Virago, 1984.

Liza's England (formerly *The Century's Daughter*). London: Virago, 1986.

The Man Who Wasn't There. London: Viking, 1988.

Regeneration. London: Viking, 1991.

The Eye in the Door. London: Viking, 1993.

The Ghost Road. London: Viking, 1995.

The Regeneration Trilogy. London: Viking, 1996. (*Regeneration*, *The Eye in the Door* and *The Ghost Road* in a single-volume edition.)

Another World. London: Viking, 1998.

Border Crossing. London: Viking, 2001.

Double Vision. London: Viking, 2003.

INT: When you began to publish did you feel that there was an indigenous working-class women's writing tradition that you could invoke?

PB: There was a distinct lack of a tradition in which I could work because although I respected the male tradition of writers like Alan Sillitoe, or the early D. H. Lawrence, for example, the women characters were quite stereotypically restricted. I always felt I was filling in the gaps of the work that came before. I wasn't continuing smoothly in a tradition and so I looked to African American writers, women such as Toni Morrison and Alice Walker, and men like James Baldwin, who were more useful to me because what I discovered in their work was the sense of an individual voice emerging out of a communal voice. There are very obvious choruses in Baldwin and Morrison's work that chimed with my own ideas about speech and dialogue. Many creative writing textbooks will tell you that each individual character is supposed to sound totally unique, and of course this is nonsense because what happens in dialogue is that people start to mirror each other, in physical positioning and gestures but also in choice of vocabulary and syntax.

One of the easy ways in which a conversation becomes collaborative is that the speakers become more and more like each other as the conversation progresses. Conversely, when relationships break down, the vocabulary and sentence structure moves further apart to emphasise the differences between the parties concerned. And there is also a sense in which the vast bulk of what human beings say to each other serves quite a primitive function by making the claim 'I am a member of the group' (the man who walks into the golf club, orders a gin and tonic and comments that the weather is nice for the time of year, for example, is signalling that he belongs). Speakers do not actually sound unique but when writing dialogue in a novel every word is carefully chosen, every nuance and every pause for breath in the space before people answer, and, if described, whether the body language concurs with or erodes what a character is saying. The dialogue in books seems like normal speech but is actually a very special sort of language, as when I was writing *Blow Your House Down* and, even though I didn't know then that I would go on to write about the First World War, I felt that the women spoke trench dialogue, the way men spoke in the trenches.

Dialogue is very important to my writing method because a novel doesn't really get going until the characters begin talking to one another and until they begin to have conversations that I don't feel I am making up, by which I mean that I feel I am listening to them as well as making them talk. They have many conversations that don't get written down; sometimes they are talking to each other and at other times I am talking to them. Once these conversations begin, the book is alive for me. Up to that point, no matter what I've written about the characters, what character analysis I may have been involved in or what notes I may have taken, there is absolutely nothing there. But I think that writers who tend to write in dialogue suffer an enormous delay in being taken seriously. It is as if there is no easy or precise critical vocabulary in which critics can talk about dialogue: they tend to comment on whether it is convincing and that's it, so you are vulnerable to being under-read. You don't have to read far into a descriptive passage by Martin Amis, for example, before you come across a startlingly brilliant figure of speech, but in a novel containing a lot of dialogue the reading experience is very different. You always come across a deceptively simple 'Yes' or 'No' and in the context of the previous twenty pages that 'Yes' or 'No' might be absolute dynamite. The effects of dialogue have to be worked up to over a long period and when they arrive they are so apparently simple.

INT: You once described dialogue to me as sculpted silence. Can you clarify that idea?

PB: I think if I were trying to teach someone to write dialogue, I would say that one of the most important things is that you start with a very powerful sense of silence, that you 'get' the silence first. When you do an interview for television, there is always the part where they record silence because that is the ambient noise out of which the words come and to which the words return and the most important thing is to be able to hear the silence. Once you hear the silence, you start sculpting the words. I think the more difficult or tense a conversation is, the more powerful the background silence has got to be. There's one of Prior's diary entries in *The Ghost Road* when he is on the Western Front and he recalls afternoons spent in therapy with Rivers and remembers that Rivers's silences were never manipulative but served to create a safe space in which Prior might speak. But he undercuts the memory by admitting that his own silences were always designed to manipulate!

INT: Dialogue is the primary site of tension in your novels, isn't it – whether cross-generational or cross-gender tensions or as bound up in the psychotherapeutic conversations your analysts have with their patients?

PB: There are two types of dialogue that fascinate me: the apparently unselfconscious, inconsequential dialogue, and the hyperconscious dialogue between a therapist and a patient where every word is loaded. Apparently inconsequential dialogue might be Lauren getting off the train in Newcastle in *Border Crossing* and stating to her husband, Tom, 'It's raining again.' He replies to the effect that it is raining everywhere and she says, with apparent simplicity, 'It wasn't raining in London.' What she actually means is 'We're getting a divorce.'

The therapist character is very present in my work but I am very critical of therapy. I thought I was sceptical but I think there is a profound distrust on my part. While I admire the people who perform therapy well, there isn't an awful lot of evidence for its success, except for brief courses of cognitive therapy where once you understand the principles, it is possible to perform a kind of autotherapy whereby one challenges oneself and one's own behavioural tendencies. On the other hand, I do believe in psychiatry for serious mental illness; I don't believe in therapy for unhappiness. Most therapists I have talked to in interviews and audiences identify with W. H. R. Rivers and castigate Tom Seymour in *Border Crossing*. Billy Prior resists therapy but turns to

Rivers all the same and I do think that Rivers's aim is for the patient to become independent of the therapist. Most psychotherapists who have talked to me about the trilogy hate the scene in which Rivers and Prior exchange seats during a session because Rivers has broken the rules. I feel that the Rivers I have created has a rock-solid sense of his own identity and while Tom Seymour loses his way as a therapist, Rivers has confidence in both knowing the rules and knowing how to break them effectively. Prior's interests and welfare come first all of the time.

INT: In *Border Crossing* you have one character dismiss the 'talking cure' as 'a whole bloody industry that doesn't do a scrap of good'; and the resistance to therapy becomes stronger in *Double Vision*, doesn't it?

PB: It does rather. Tom in *Border Crossing* is not an effective therapist in the case of Danny Miller and in *Double Vision* there is an explicit rejection of therapy on Stephen's part, and on Kate's really. She repudiates what is conventionally thought to be the long drawn-out restorative process of healing, which is a reaction to grief I have noted. If you really love the dead person, you don't actually want to recover, so to have grief represented as recovery from an illness is not a helpful metaphor at all. She finds amputation more helpful because it is permanent but adaptable to relatively quickly. Stephen repudiates the potential label of Post-Traumatic Stress Disorder – not that he doesn't think he fits it but because he doesn't think the label will help him to get better. In the end he too adapts to a sort of secular or aesthetic equivalent for healing through thinking about how Goya managed.

And there is something in Danny Miller that is perhaps impossible to deal with, in therapy or outside of it. By *Double Vision*, he has almost become that in human nature which we find impossible to accept. There is also a shift away from the psychotherapeutic conversation you have talked about. In *Double Vision* Peter Wingrave's weapons have become entirely physical. In *Border Crossing* Danny Miller manipulates through speech, whereas in his new incarnation as Peter he manipulates others aesthetically or through his movements: the way he touches or doesn't touch Kate or the sculpture as they work together and the way he seems to commandeer Kate's identity when he wears her clothes. In fact, he is virtually silent for much of *Double Vision*.

I don't believe you can overturn the first ten years of your life – that is, your basic personality structure – through therapy, although cognitive therapy can be useful partly because it explicitly refuses to understand the root of the problem only in terms of the past. I also don't think you can unlearn the basic grammar that is inbuilt when we are young. I am often surprised at how my own language structure is not middle class except when I am trying to convey the thought processes of a character who is born middle class. The poet Georg Szirtes, who spoke Hungarian until he was five when he came to Britain as a refugee, tells a story that bears this out. By his late thirties he was returning to Hungary but had no memory of the Hungarian language and knew he would have to learn it anew but he found that he knew the grammar, the syntax; and that interests me, that the deep structure of the language was embedded so early.

INT:　Would you say you write cautionary tales?

PB:　In some senses I suppose I do. One of the things we should be cautious about is labelling. There is the risk to the individuality of the person being categorised. I can see that from the point of view of training people to be psychiatrists, or psychiatrists talking meaningfully to each other, there have to be labels; you cannot work on the basis of the individual patient, it has to be on the basis of such labels or descriptors. I can quite see that a very experienced and talented clinician can fully respond to the individual humanity of the patient, whilst, at the same time, running through a list of questions which will enable him or her to reach a diagnosis. However, in my books I refuse to label Danny Miller and I question the label of Asperger's Syndrome attached to Adam. Is a very bright kid who behaves oddly best served in this way? I watched a television documentary recently narrated by a young man with Asperger's Syndrome for whom the label was a relief because it explained why his peers had shunned him as a geek and a freak but I am not sure whether the label actually helps. It has been said of Wittgenstein and Einstein that they suffered from Asperger's – the upper end of autism, if you like – but there seems to be a certain vanity in labelling in this way: instead of recognising transcendent achievement, we stick a label on it to account for it and demean them.

INT: So retrospective labelling is about confining people and conditions to a manageable discourse?

PB: To an extent, as with shellshock: a label I examine in *Regeneration*; or with writers themselves. I have always thought it limiting and unsophisticated to read fiction solely through the prism of autobiography, with the author's life like a picked-over carcass. Looking for whatever parallels there may possibly be with the author's life also leads to under-reading the fiction.

Danny is a murderer but he has no real memory of the crucial thing he needs to remember – the missing hours he spent with Lizzie's corpse after he killed her. He is in such a disintegrated state in the immediate aftermath of killing her (not when he killed her, necessarily) that in the missing five hours no memories were being laid down that could be recovered. What is interesting, then, is that he will imagine something into the gap, especially if questioned about it. It is too uncomfortable to admit the gap – the irretrievable time – and so those involved suppose what must have happened is what did happen. But I don't let Danny invent the events in any detail: he cannot face them. The reader doesn't know what Danny does or doesn't know about himself, except through what he says, and he is such a good liar. The gap at the heart of *Border Crossing* was a conscious decision – it's like Room 101 really, the worst thing in the world. What *did* he do to Lizzie? But, then, he can't have done very much because he left so little evidence. In any case, the effect on him is devastating but seeking the truth involves peeling away layers of lies. I didn't want to confine the character so that the reader can manage him easily.

INT: Danny Miller cannot retrieve his own aberrant moment as a killer; but do you return the reader to the historical past so often in your books because we are basically an amnesiac culture and do not learn society's lessons well?

PB: I think that is true and that shellshock is an interesting case in point. It is striking that a greater openness about fear in war is generally attributed to the Falklands or the first Gulf War in recent discussion, as if to distinguish what has been learned from the mistakes of treating soldiers returning from earlier wars like the Vietnam War. It would seem that the participants in television or other discussions are unaware of the key articles published in the *Lancet* in 1917 and the work Rivers and others undertook at the beginning of the twentieth century. Perhaps with medicine the advances are so rapid that insights are lost as well as gained with the passage of time.

I think much of my own sense of time derives from being brought up by the generation before my parents, by people old enough to return to the past in the way elderly people do, and hearing my great aunts quarrelling about what happened on a particular day in 1911 because the past still mattered passionately. Our memory in old age turns on the past, and what also interests me is that instead of the environment having a greater and greater effect on you as you age, your genetic endowment becomes clearer; so when women feel that they are turning into their mothers, they actually are becoming more like a parent. The past resolves in the present because the genes are inside you working themselves out and continue to express themselves in the future.

In the trilogy, Rivers does believe in recovering the past, both for himself in terms of his drive to recover whatever event destroyed his visual memory, and for his patients. I also think about returning to the past as bearing witness: when Njiru knows his people are lost in *The Ghost Road* he tells the words of the exorcism to Rivers because he realises his words will survive whereas if he tells them to his own people, a society that is dying, his words may be lost. So his words and the exorcism both survive and do not survive in the novel: the oral tradition is lost but the story survives.

INT: Is he like Liza in *Liza's England* in her relationship with a surrogate son, Stephen?

PB: I hadn't thought of that; their contexts are so different. But Njiru and Liza do have things in common: they cannot perform the natural passing on of culture through their descendants because that process has been blocked for both of them, so they find other conduits. Stephen listens to Liza but he doesn't listen to his own father, his own family story. The quasi-parental relationship which recurs in my books overlaps with the therapy relationship as well.

I think the idea of *how* we remember also surfaces very forcefully in *Another World* and in particular in the character of Geordie. He is overwhelmed by his memory of his brother Harry's death and memory paradoxically delivers him to a time that is always present:

that stops being the past because it takes place in an unending present tense. What I was trying to do in that novel, I think, was to put together two different theories about the way people remember: at one extreme, what Geordie is permitted or encouraged to remember of the war is virtually dictated to him by the society in which he lives. On the other hand, there is the chemistry of the brain and ideas like Post-Traumatic Stress Disorder. That response would not be modified by subsequent learning and is a non-verbal record; it is a silent record, because it is a part of the brain which is too primitive to be able to utilise language, so it gets back to the idea of silence. I was trying to put those two ideas together. In the 1920s, Geordie can't say that the war was a waste but in the 1960s he certainly can. In the end, though, he is undoubtedly influenced by society, but society does not touch those core memories that continue to haunt him, which are actually the core of his identity.

INT: So research forms a significant part of your thinking as you begin to write?

PB: I was thinking about some of the work being undertaken by neurobiologists on memory with *Another World* but I wouldn't want to write a book directly out of specific research; I didn't want to interview psychotherapists before creating the therapist Tom Seymour in *Border Crossing*, for example. Rather, he evolves as a character in my mind. Research can be shared with others in a way that the idea of a novel as it develops can't be shared with anyone, until it has progressed to a stage where it can be shared. Until then you are very much alone. I do like to research my novels in terms of the coming together of assorted strands that contribute to the ideas. *The Ghost Road* would have been an easier book for me to write if I had excised the Melanesians, but I didn't see the point of writing an anti-war novel that only examined the tragedy that is already part of the fabric of our national consciousness, men dying on the Western Front. Their tragedy had to be counterpointed by the society in the Baring Straits dying from the absence of war because it has been the purpose of their lives.

I have toyed with the idea of a split-level book with a Victorian or Edwardian strand and a contemporary one. In the former there is a governess living in the hinterland between servants and the family they serve. I had been reading *The Victorian Governess* by Catherine

Hughes and long before that I read Charlotte Brontë's letters and, of course, *Jane Eyre*. Then I noticed that a teacher in Newcastle had the idea of staging a fashion show with her pupils dressed in Edwardian costumes but that none of the slim teenage girls at the beginning of the twenty-first century could fit into the clothing: they were too big. I began to put ideas of space and form together and remembered that in Toronto I had stayed at the Edward VII Hotel where there is a painting of him in Coronation robes, his huge chest spreading out over the canvas as if to take up as much space as possible. In the contemporary strand there is an anorexic school-phobic girl and ideas of space and confinement begin to ferment. The Victorian governess's confinement is not of her own making but sociological, whereas the anorexic girl has pathologically confined herself to home. How sociological is her plight? What are we doing to girls who have more confined lives than they were obliged to in the Victorian past? Such ideas feed back into my general reading around eating disorders, confinement and exclusion. So 'research' is a real mix – from painting to books read twenty years ago and others read more recently.

INT: The girls you describe in the hypothetical story occupy liminal spaces. You have a tendency to think in terms of liminality – not margins exactly because the characters are not always at the edges of society – but between social groups, or between one class and another?

PB: Yes, the space the governess occupies belongs neither with the family nor the servants. She therefore has a unique vantage point precisely because of her experience in the little room she occupies between stairs from which she sees everything. In this she is a little like Prior in the trilogy perhaps, 'neither fish nor fowl'. Point of view is important and the character I focused on when first conceiving of this possible story had much more space within the setting and was more central to it. But I wanted a different point of view. The seemingly simple question 'Whose story is this?' can be very complicated and it is not always the obvious character who comes to the fore.

Writing *Double Vision* I played with the idea of making Kate the central character, but I veered towards Stephen and the structuring principle of shifting the point of view part way through the novel because what is happening to Kate via her battle to create the Christ image is so internalised that it would make it difficult to locate her as the book's central character. I did play with ways of doing that. At one point she was attacked and at another she and Stephen had an affair. There were alternative versions of the book you have read. But in the end, I thought what was right for Kate was a celibate, monastic existence, a very lonely struggle to create this gigantic human chrysalis which is also a form of defiance of this difficult emotional chapter of her life. Stephen looks out into the world and she looks inward, although she is very aware also of the kinds of images that others like Ben and Stephen bring back from the outside world. Kate and Stephen are two viewpoint characters thinking about similar problems of representation; but she is grappling with the practicalities of how you get the balance in the actual work while he grapples with the second-hand character of the images of what he has experienced in covering wars as a journalist.

INT: How did *Double Vision* develop as a novel?

PB: The novel really started with the character of Stephen Sharkey, the war correspondent, and my being present at Slobodan Milosevic's International War Crime Tribunal at The Hague in February 2002, and more generally with photographs and images of war. It started almost with another book – the one Stephen is writing in the novel – on how we represent war, and it developed through that. What came to me early on was the episode in Sarajevo where at the heart of a city at war you have a crime, a rape and murder. Although, of course, the rape may be politically motivated and therefore a war crime, it was the linking of criminality and war that preoccupied me. Are there in fact any differences between 'legitimate' violence in war and the 'illegitimate' violence of crime? There is a bridge of violence between the two that is becoming more and more blurred. The climax of the plot in *Double Vision* is a totally random act of crime and you aren't supposed to 'resolve' novels in this way; but I wanted this act to be left random in terms of the book's structure and therefore particularly difficult to accept, as acts of violence often are when havens of safety are subject to incursions. The random act develops out of my interest in social pathologies. So the book started with ideas around legitimate and illegitimate violence but also with the character watching the trial developing conjunctivitis – a condition where the eyes are inflamed is obviously a very appropriate thing for Stephen to be suffering from. I attended the trial as I was beginning the novel and it was a fascinating process, especially in terms of the image of Milosevic. We saw a distorted image of the man through a bullet-proof screen behind which I sat with the journalists and human rights activists and the rest of the onlookers, and above us was a television screen which produced a much clearer close-up image. The screen image was much more informative than the image of the real man in the courtroom.

INT: So the most autobiographical experience that finds its way into the novel is actually one in which you are commenting, interpreting, examining the experience critically.

PB: Yes, perhaps the idea of 'double vision' again. My experience did not mirror Stephen's in the novel. Although I watched the trial, the character's approach to it is fundamentally different from mine: he is a journalist and such experiences are often assignments so he has a context that I do not, although, of course, in another sense the Milosevic trial was a new experience, even for seasoned journalists. I didn't go to see Vermeer's *Girl with a Pearl Earring*, although I knew the painting was there in the Mauritshuis museum in The Hague, but it was important for the character to see it: the painting reminds him of Justine, the much younger woman with whom he is beginning a relationship. Danny and Peter became identified at a comparatively late stage: they were similar characters rather than the same character when the novel was conceived. In *Double Vision* the community may be small but the scene has broadened for Peter, and the other characters are more capable of resisting him than in *Border Crossing*; he is a dark patch in an overall picture. And insofar as the whole book is concerned with keeping the balance, he is much better balanced by the other characters then he ever could be by Tom Seymour whom he takes over. I like the idea of the comparative lack of altruism of Stephen and Kate and, indeed, Justine, though she is more altruistic than either of them. It is this which protects them from Peter, paradoxically.

INT: *Double Vision* is the first novel in which you concentrate on an almost entirely rural setting and it is your most middle-class novel too. Why the shift?

PB: There is far more emphasis on landscape as a personality (rather like the army hospital Craiglockhart in *Regeneration*). I wasn't particularly aware as I began to write that the landscape would become so important, but then Northern England has the largest forest area in

England. If you stand in the centre of the woods, especially in the middle of winter, you can feel how ancient it is but also something intrinsically terrifying. In many different ways the novel undercuts the English pastoral myth – the Forest of Arden – that the rural retreat is inevitably healing. Although Stephen learns to love the landscape, the rural England he retreats to is in deep crisis through the foot and mouth epidemic that has left its scars on the landscape as well as financially and socially, and rural crime, and the crisis fed by people buying up cottages and farmhouses and squeezing out the local young people who would otherwise be living in them. It is a picture of depredation and Stephen heals himself in spite not because of it. One of the books that was in my mind was V. S. Naipaul's brilliant *The Enigma of Arrival*, in which he is setting off to walk to Stonehenge and feels that he is the lone foreigner in an unchanging world only to discover as he penetrates deeper into that world that it is in continual flux and will absorb him as it has absorbed everything else. I had that book in mind when I wrote about the myth of the soldier returning to an unchanged landscape.

Double Vision is my most middle-class book, as you say, with characters who work in the city but choose to live in the countryside. One minor character called Angela refers to the 'green-welly Christians' up for the weekend and the middle-class newcomers are generally parasitical, except for Beth who does make a contribution to the local community. The predicament of the vicar is fascinating to me and you don't have to be a believer to find his role interesting in the way that David Hare has too, for example. The vicar is in the community but not of it and he is conflicted over his repressed aggression, his sexuality, his vanity and belief, but he also has a genuine spirituality and a deep moral sense. In one scene, a Sunday lunch, Beth is trying to make the community work as she thinks it *should* while relying on another character, Justine, to carry the practicalities of cooking for the occasion. It is perhaps the most expressive scene of the mêlée of middle-class characters in the novel and Beth is trying to regiment them.

INT: Would you call yourself a novelist of ideas?

PB: It is a phrase my publisher has used and it has been used about me, but the label 'novelist of ideas' means that ideas drive the book and for me they don't. Novels of ideas are easiest to talk about in many ways but my books are character-driven and I hope that the characters embody a complex of ideas and have their own ideas as well. I would always say that if you write a novel about characters sitting around a table discussing free will, it is not a novel about free will but about sitting around a table. I don't like characters that function as mouthpieces: the only ideas that matter in a novel are the ideas which find expression in the choices characters make under pressure and in the actions they take as a result of those choices. What the characters talk about may or may not be the subject of the book, and very frequently isn't. You read many so-called 'novels of ideas' where the ideas are only there at the level of conversation and that simply doesn't count. I suppose any label – the novelist of ideas, or the feminist or working-class or Northern writer – are epithets you bounce off and refuse to have attached to you, labels you walk away from as fast as you can! For me, the fact that I switched the gender perspective in my work at the same time as I changed publisher compounded the issue of labelling. By the time I left Virago there was a backlog of things I wanted to explore about men, but then further down the line it came to be assumed that I no longer wrote about women. As you know, I have never divided men and women characters in this way and it is interesting to me that some people couldn't really conceive of foregrounding the voices of women as *not* being hostile to men – and vice versa.

INT: Why are you interested in creating chameleon characters – Colin Harper in *The Man Who Wasn't There*, Billy Prior, Danny Miller – young men who are disturbing and strange?

PB: There is an attempt to grapple with evil figures in my work, as with the rapist and murderer in *Blow Your House Down*. I wanted to be able to get into his mind very briefly, but while I was in his mind to make him a completely credible and completely terrifying figure. The murder was an enormous challenge: to make a man credible who was essentially torturing another human being to death. I wanted the reader to feel that if you were alone with that man, you would be alone with somebody whom you couldn't reach emotionally by any means whatsoever. But I didn't then want him to dominate; I wanted the women to come back to the centre of the stage. Billy Prior, on the other hand, is so vigorous that he's a breath of life; he's a very energetic character to write. He suffers fugue states in *The Eye in the*

Door, splits in his personality, yet he retains a strong sense of his identity, I think. He's very curious: the pressures on him are so enormous that he can't stay in touch with all of himself all the time. But he refuses to be limited; he has a willingness to experiment across sexual, social and national boundaries and, of course, his genesis lies in his ability to irritate another character. His sole function in the beginning was to be exactly the kind of character that the historical Rivers might find difficult and he grew from there.

The chameleon in Prior is not evil. For example, he is both mute *and* fakes mutism in *Regeneration*, and in *The Ghost Road* there is the false medium, Njiru, who also knows how to fake divination. Billy Prior can fake and feint but Danny Miller is something else again: he is frightening and calculating. He is a chilling character. To begin with in *Border Crossing*, you have the working out of his destructive parasitic probing, but with the balance of power radically changed from that of Prior and Rivers in the trilogy. Once he emerges as Peter Wingrave in *Double Vision* it becomes clear that he has been to this village before when newly released from prison into an interim safe house, when Justine was a child, and that he has returned and asked the vicar Alec for a breathing space; but the reason for this is withheld. However, he is not such a chameleon character that he could live in a rural setting: he would be too much an object of curiosity whereas in a large city he can pass unremarked. He, of course, lives in the city and works in the country so he is always moving in the opposite direction to the other characters (as Robert goes to the hospital or Stephen to work on his book in the university library). There are other ways in which he can pass, of course. Little Adam could not pass as anything other than what he is whereas Peter is incapable of remaining what he is; he is so fluid a character that he has the opposite problem to Adam, who is a professorial little boy who sticks out in any classroom or context and cannot do anything about the fact because he is unable to judge others' reactions to him. Peter, in a surface kind of way, can slot into society and make superficial relationships at least because he is a virtuoso of other people's reactions. Adam can never merge with another person in the way that Peter does. But Peter's merging is not real intimacy or communion because you need a sense of your difference from the other person and in that secure separation you may approach a deeply intimate friendship. Peter is the atom who clings to other atoms.

INT: Is there much consolation in this book, do you think? I can see glimmers of hope for many of the characters but not for Danny Miller/Peter Wingrave.

PB: He has stayed out of prison but he has been dealt a hand of cards he can never play successfully. He is becoming a creative writer but should he be judged by the short stories he writes in which a prisoner is proved incapable of rehabilitation or redemption? It is back to the old chestnut – how far does it help you to understand their stories if you know about the person writing them? This idea takes us back to the journalistic probing of writers' lives when the questions asked have little relation to the work or the creative process. If Peter were to publish and become successful, he might be a crime writer who had actually killed, a celebrity of a sort, but he is not allowed to profit from his crime. He has to keep himself remote from others and he does so, except for Justine in a relationship he cannot maintain.

INT: What about despair and consolation as a writerly dilemma?

PB: I like the idea of the dilemma at the heart of the writing, as in the first chapter of Ian McEwan's *Enduring Love*, that awful scene in which the characters run towards a catastrophe: the hot air balloon with a child aboard. The men make up a microcosm of a society that tries to save the young boy in the balloon's basket. If they all haul together, the balloon may be returned to earth but unless they all let go together the most altruistic man who keeps hold of the rope will die. Perhaps in *Double Vision* the closest you come to a hint of what might be some kind of consolation is when Kate is in the Bowes Museum looking at Goya's picture of the seven prisoners, a picture that expresses despair; but she feels a dual response – the depths of despair combining with a kind of joy that a human being is capable of creating this and, once again, it is a double vision of what art can do. You cannot create out of total despair, which is why it is important for the writer not to offer a completely despairing response to the universe. It may be the correct response but it is not a truthful account of what the writer or artist feels when writing their poem or creating their painting. If you are creating you have hope.

Select criticism

■ Books

Jolly, Margaretta, Sharon Monteith, Ronald Paul and Nahem Yousaf, eds. *Critical Perspectives on Pat Barker*. Columbia: University of South Carolina Press, 2005.

Monteith, Sharon. *Pat Barker*. London: Northcote House, 2002.

Westman, Karin. *Pat Barker's Regeneration: A Readers' Guide*. New York and London: Continuum, 2001.

■ Articles

Ardis, Ann. 'Political Attentiveness vs. Political Correctness: Teaching Pat Barker's *Blow Your House Down*', *College Literature* 18: 3 (Oct. 1991), pp. 44–54.

Harris, Greg. 'Compulsory Masculinity, Britain and the Great War: The Literary-Historical Work of Pat Barker', *Critique: Studies in Contemporary Fiction* 39: 2 (June 1998), pp. 290–304.

Hitchcock, Peter. 'Radical Writing' in *Dialogics of the Oppressed*. Minneapolis: University of Minnesota Press, 1993, pp. 53–82.

Jolly, Margaretta. 'After Feminism: Pat Barker, Penelope Lively and the Contemporary Novel' in Alan Sinfield and Alastair Davies, eds, *British Culture of the Post War: An Introduction to Literature and Society 1945–1999*. London: Routledge, 2000.

Kirk, John. 'Recovered Perspectives: Gender, Class and Memory in Pat Barker's Writing', *Contemporary Literature* 40: 4 (Winter 1999), pp. 603–26.

Mukherjee, Ankhi. 'Stammering to Story: Neurosis and Narration in Pat Barker's *Regeneration*', *Critique: Studies in Contemporary Fiction* 43: 1 (Fall 2001), pp. 49–62.

Newman, Jenny. 'Souls and Arseholes: The Double Vision of *Liza's England*', *Critical Survey* 13: 1 (2001), pp. 18–36.

Pykett, Lyn. '*The Century's Daughters:* Recent Women's Fiction and History', *Critical Quarterly* 29: 3 (Autumn 1987), pp. 71–7.

Ross, Michael. 'Acts of Revision: Lawrence as Intertext in the Novels of Pat Barker', *D.H. Lawrence Review* 26: 1–3 (1995), pp. 51–63.

2 A. S. Byatt

James Friel and Jenny Newman

A. S. Byatt is one of today's most ambitious novelists and short-story writers, redeploying the complex narrative strategies of the great Victorians, especially George Eliot. Committed to the 'novel of ideas', Byatt also describes herself as a realist, albeit consciously so. With its diverse cast, complex plot and refusal to limit itself to a single viewpoint, her recently completed *The Quartet* allows her not only to follow her characters from 1953 to 1970 and beyond, but also to chronicle conflicts and trends in spheres such as education, biology, religion, television and the arts, in both London and the provinces. Byatt broke from its demands to write *Possession* (1990), which won the Booker Prize and the Irish Times/Aer Lingus International Fiction Prize. It incorporates critical theory, satirised – often with amused affection – through Byatt's accounts of rival groups of British and American scholars. Part literary detective story, part pastiche and part Gothic thriller, *Possession* is subtitled *A Romance*, and each of its parallel plots has its love affair: one between the 'Victorian' poets Christabel LaMotte and Randolph Henry Ash, and the other between two of the twentieth-century critics and scholars who study and become 'possessed' by them.

In *Babel Tower*, the third novel of *The Quartet*, Byatt continues to manipulate contrasting discourses – here academic, journalistic, biological, legal – to both comic and sinister effect. She also continues the story of brilliant, egocentric Frederica Potter, and of her younger brother, Marcus. Now in his twenties, he is depicted as one of a group of biologists at work on the Yorkshire moors, investigating genetic memory in snails, an aspect of Byatt's longstanding fascination with biology, and a comment on the moral world of her novel.

Through her virtuoso use of the omniscient narrator, Byatt has developed a capacious yet flexible narrative style, and her characters' feelings, actions and thoughts are often linked to contemporary issues and events. Although she describes herself as an atheist, she allows some of her characters to approach an almost mystical awareness of the physical world's meaning and structure. Byatt has become a prolific commentator on the metropolitan literary scene, but most of her novels at some point revisit Yorkshire, and she draws on her knowledge of its earth even when writing about the Cévennes, in France, where she spends her summers, and where Yorkshire becomes what she calls 'an analogical hook'. She was appointed a CBE in 1990 and a DBE in 1999.

Key works

■ Novels and novellas

The Shadow of the Sun. London: Chatto & Windus, 1964.

The Game. London: Chatto & Windus, 1967.

The Virgin in the Garden. London: Chatto & Windus, 1978.

Still Life. London: Chatto & Windus, 1985.

Possession: A Romance. London: Chatto & Windus, 1990.

Angels and Insects. London: Chatto & Windus, 1992.

Babel Tower. London: Chatto & Windus, 1996.

The Biographer's Tale. London: Chatto & Windus, 2000.

A Whistling Woman. London: Chatto & Windus, 2002.

The Quartet (omnibus). London: Chatto & Windus, 2003.

■ Short stories

Sugar and Other Stories. London: Chatto & Windus, 1987.

The Matisse Stories. London: Chatto & Windus, 1993.

The Djinn in the Nightingale's Eye. London: Chatto & Windus, 1994.

Elementals: Stories of Fire and Ice. London: Chatto & Windus, 1998.

Collected Stories. London: Chatto & Windus, 2000.

The Little Black Book of Stories. London: Chatto & Windus, 2003.

INT: In your essay 'Memory and the Making of Fiction' you quote George Eliot's description of childhood memory as 'a sweet habit of the blood'. Do your childhood memories relate to your beginnings as a writer?

ASB: There are two kinds of memories, at least in my case: firstly, memories of *things*, about half a dozen things that are part of my very early childhood, which in a curious way seem to be part of me as a writer. There was a cast iron stove with the brand name 'Tiger Stove', and I could see it wasn't a tiger or a stove. There was also a certain walk we used to go on when we lived in Pontefract, which I remember with a pleasure which is verbal because my mother came with us. She wasn't terribly good at doing things with children, but she told me the name of every flower, both Latin and English, as we walked along the road. There's always something verbal behind my early memories which is more than a mnemonic; it's me being excited by language.

I spend a lot of my time wondering why human beings ever invented metaphor, and why they bother to make works of art. You know, why don't they just get on with their lives? I think the answers to both questions are involved with each other. We get a kind of physiological excitement when two threads of the mind cross. Because the Tiger Stove wasn't a tiger or a stove it somehow caused a fizzing in my brain, and I think I make works of art to repeat that excitement.

INT: In *The Virgin in the Garden* you look back at Elizabethan England through a series of flower metaphors.

ASB: I finished that book in Gladstone's library, where I found a Victorian book of flower names and got excited by the metaphoric structure of the names of the grasses that Marcus was looking at, so I put them all in the novel. It's obviously a deep, human excitement, because every three or four years I get a letter saying, 'By the way, I do like the metaphorical flower names.'

INT: Don't you also associate a direct, non-metaphorical relationship between word and thing with the Edenic state?

ASB: In my PhD thesis I wrote about a theory we then believed in called 'the dissociation of sensibility', which was an imagined point in time when words ceased to be interwoven with things. Foucault wrote about it at length in the 1980s; but English-language criticism was thinking it out in the 1950s.

I've been asked to give a lecture in New York about a work of art which affected me as an artist and I've chosen 'The Ancient Mariner', which is, in a way, an answer to the questions we've so far discussed. Coleridge has an obsession with words which were things. I've been thinking how 'ice mast-high went floating by, as green as emerald', which I associate with the transparent green boiled sweets my paternal grandfather used to make. When I read about the ice and the snow and the water and the sun and the moon in 'The Ancient Mariner', it was like living in a mythic world; so I want to talk about how scholarship intensifies this excitement, rather than diminishing it.

INT: That excitement could have led you to become a linguist or a philosopher. To have become a novelist and found ways of dramatising those ideas, you must have had a great interest in telling stories.

ASB: I used to think, like George Eliot, that I wasn't a born storyteller. When Eliot started writing, George Henry Lewes said his one doubt was whether she could tell a story. He knew she could do all the other things, but in those days nobody thought that the novel could do all those other things! I knew I ought to write a novel, but I grew up at the time when E. M. Forster said, 'Oh dear, yes, the novel tells a story.' That was one thing we were being told not to do through most of my apprenticeship as a novelist. I thought it was a rather vulgar gift compared to Virginia Woolf's, or Wordsworth's or Coleridge's, and that it should be abolished or kept down if one had it. Then I realised that actually you owe people stories.

There's also a cussedness that makes you, if you get hold of one end of any stick, want to go right to the other end of it. You don't want to stop in the middle, or say, 'Well, that will do now. I know enough about that.' My first editor was Cecil Day-Lewis, and he used to talk most beautifully about Wordsworth's Highland girl singing, and say how important it was for Wordsworth to stop listening. Well, I can't stop. Cecil would stop when he found an image he could use. Then he could say, 'I don't want to know any more.' But I would go ferreting on and ferreting on. Usually it produced something much more interesting, but it was very tiring!

INT: With Ignês Sodré, you speak about novels you read and study, and think and dream about: a way of reading a book which is almost a life's work. Is that the way you wish to be read?

ASB: I do want to be read like that, and feel that professional criticism over the last twenty years has made it harder, not easier, to read a book with the whole of yourself and the whole of your body, to be what I call a 'greedy reader'. I'm worried about the increasingly judgemental element teachers introduce into the reading process: we have these techniques which mean we know better than the writer does what the writer is doing. With highly complex French theorists this may be true with some of the writers they choose, but mostly I don't believe it. Readers should be empowered to skip, which sounds simple but isn't. They now read every word, and feel they should always be forming a judgement; whereas I never review a book without reading it through first very fast. I will make a note of what strikes me but won't expect to have a thought. You just read it to see if you *can* read it – in all senses of the word 'can', including whether it interests you – and, of course, at this stage in my life, if I can't read it, I don't.

If you don't see art as being profoundly related to the pleasure principle there's something wrong with you. Art is not there for making sociological observations or political decisions or, really, to be a substitute for psychoanalysis; though the great novelists are wiser than most politicians, most sociologists and most psychoanalysts, except the very great ones of all those. I think that, while Martin Amis feels it is required of the modern novelist to write something about the atom bomb, it probably isn't. We're all afraid of it and it will come in at the edges of whatever we write. What we in this country feel about war with Iraq is for a great journalist to take on, not for me as a novelist. What one offers the reader is a much more slow and complicated relationship with an individual habit of mind.

I want my readers to want to read and reread me, and if they don't quite understand, ask themselves, 'Now why the hell is it snails she's interested in?' I get letters all the time, and particularly from America, saying, 'I thought your Victorian poets were real, and I looked them up and found they didn't exist, but I did get out Tennyson and Browning, and, dear Mrs Byatt, can I tell you what pleasure I got out of *The Idylls of the King*, which I was told I should never read because it's a very bad poem.' I like to spark people on to reading another thing and another thing.

There's nothing wrong with being consumable on the surface, which I was taught there was. It was meant to be absolutely wonderful to be as difficult as Robbe-Grillet, because that was a sign of authenticity. I think Gabriel Jospovici still believes that a kind of resistance to easy reading is a guarantee of a novel's merit. But all sorts of great things have an aspect which is easily graspable. You can read almost all my books as though they were just romantic novels. That's also true of George Eliot, Dickens and Dostoevsky, and even of Proust, if you've got the staying power. It's true of Lawrence Norfolk, who is the best of the young novelists now writing.

I would like my readers to take me on trust, which is difficult in the present academic climate. It isn't what Coleridge meant by a suspension of disbelief, but I need them to suspend judgement until they have a sense of how the novel fits together. I have an image that Walter Jackson Bate used about Keats: the bird in the nest with its mouth open for more and then more and then more. There's a woman who says that every time she finishes one of my books she immediately starts again! That's what one wants, people who reread one's books.

At the moment I'm joyfully rereading Balzac. One can reread George Eliot; and I go on rereading Jane Austen. I knew her by heart before I was a teenager, and yet when I open one of her novels I read one sentence and then another. She didn't write in order to be against slavery, though I'm sure she was a good woman and like most intelligent English people at the time she was against it. But that isn't the point: the point is telling a story that is better than other people's stories, and more compulsive.

INT: Do you see yourself as a religious novelist?

ASB: I'm an agnostic, and always have been, and have had no experience that I would describe as religious as opposed to aesthetic. I had a strong religious upbringing, because I was sent to a Quaker school, and Quakers have a religion which is accessible to irreligious people because it's a form of contemplative silence and real morality. The other thing is that if you have read literature as I did, you see that the world I grew up in was a Christian world. Even people who didn't think they were Christian had Christian points of reference and ways of expressing their morals. I don't think I knew anything about Judaism when I was young, but, insofar as Judaism is the Old Testament, it is subsumed. This is no longer true, and we don't know the source of our moral authority. I try to write religious novels about that.

The person who understood that was Iris Murdoch, but she would have liked Christianity to have been true if it could. I never believed it was true. If something isn't true, you should jettison it, even if you find yourself in a cold, dangerous, empty place. On the other hand, in place of a religious framework, we have taken to using reality television and celebrity gossip, and a dreadfully exhausting interest in our own personality. Nobody has written a novel about that, and so far we haven't got a climate in which novelists can see right round it all.

INT: Do you see Freud as the source of that interest in the workings of our minds?

ASB: I'm talking about something much less beautiful than Freud, because he carries the whole of European culture with him: the classics, Judaism and Christianity. Frankly, I find it boring as I get older when people discuss their personalities with me, because they do very much resemble each other! It must have been interesting to be a Father Confessor, because he had certain parameters. A sin you hadn't met would be fascinating.

I do miss the cosmic dimension to the sense of what it is to be human. Marcus in *The Virgin in the Garden* is a self-portrait: somebody baffled by things being far too much and not fittable into any of the languages you were offered. I can recognise 'The Ancient Mariner' for what it is: a cosmic poem of no religion. It's on the edge of Coleridge deciding for Christianity but, whatever he thought it was, it's not Christian: it's about strangeness.

INT: When *Possession* was published in 1990 you were in the middle of a quartet. *The Virgin in the Garden* had appeared in 1978, and *Still Life* in 1985, but with *Babel Tower* and *A Whistling Woman* still to come, the quartet was taking you some time to complete.

ASB: Most of the gap was caused by the death of my son. I went to teach at University College simply to pay his school fees, and he got killed the week I accepted the job. I wouldn't have otherwise become a teacher; I wanted to become a writer. Added to which I was pregnant, so the slowness of the novels, given a full-time university job, a new baby and a dead child can be put as a flat, autobiographical narrative. Quite how I survived and went on thinking I don't know, but I instinctively made the right decision because I knew the students would keep me alive, as I couldn't at that stage keep myself alive. Teaching them Coleridge and Milton and John Donne kept me going. Also, being in University College caused me to have the sort of thoughts I had in *Possession* which I otherwise might not have had. There were two things going on in my mind: one was that I knew that *Babel Tower* ought to be a parodic novel in several voices, and I thought that I wasn't technically skilled enough. Also, I had planned to kill Stephanie before my son had died. I thought almost every day that I wouldn't go on with that, because it was too much. Nevertheless, it was unfinished business, so I did it.

INT: Do you see *Possession* as a Rubicon in your career as a writer?

ASB: I see it as a comedy, although it makes people cry. That's nothing to do with me at all; it's about those primitive pleasures we were talking about, the tiger stove, and metaphor and language. I stopped teaching in 1984, and thought that if I started a novel just for pleasure I would learn how to write much faster and write the novel that I now wanted to write as opposed to one that I had planned twenty years earlier. It liberated me, not just because it was a success but because the words fell into place.

INT: You've talked about not being a poet, but in *Possession* you liberated yourself into poetry.

ASB: Yes, and they all tried not to publish it. No American publisher would take it for ages, and the English publishers tried to make me take all the poetry out – and when they failed they pretended they never had! I was doubtful about it. It was more than ventriloquism; it was a sort of a homage to Browning and Tennyson, then Coleridge, and Milton far behind them. I was saying how much I loved them. I thought Ash's poem ought to be about Swammerdam, who comes in the preface to the *Comédie Humaine*. I wrote down a few metaphors and just ran at it and wrote the poem instead of writing an essay on an imaginary poem, which is how I'd first conceived *Possession* – I'd thought there would be a lot of, as it were, spoof essays. Then I saw that the novel ought to be in what I think of now as C major, in that there should be real poems. I thought about Christina Rossetti and decided that I really don't like her, so had a go at Emily Dickinson. I managed to combine them and make a whole new person.

INT: Do you see your own texts as gendered?

ASB: I've played with trying to understand what the word means, but use either 'sex' or 'men and women' instead, partly because the word 'gendered' has caused many of my friends to write work that is bordering on not saying anything. I have always had a romantic idea that the writer or the artist was, as Coleridge and Virginia Woolf said, androgynous. The whole of *The Virgin in the Garden* quartet is about the desirability of an androgynous mind.

I am too old for the women's movement in America or this country. I was fighting battles for the freedom of women, all by myself as I saw it, in the fifties. I was partly amazed by the organised fight and partly appalled, because freedoms it had been hard for us to win – to be taken seriously by men as equal people to talk to – were suddenly thrown away by the idea that women should band together and talk to each other about each other, about women, and have Women's Studies in women's buildings.

I learnt never to write a list of my favourite painters or writers without women in, but, equally, I would never write one without men in. I don't think you can live in the world if the battle between the sexes is more important than communication between the sexes. It never was, to me – I like men. My father was one of the most important presences in my life, and he was rational and sane and liked women.

What Hélène Cixous does is fine for Cixous but it doesn't get me very far. You can't play the kind of games that she and Lacan play in a language like English which isn't gendered in its ordinary nouns. The moon in French is feminine, in German masculine, in English neuter. We think about things as things, because we have a neuter. The interesting thing about French is that it is a language with only one source, which is Romance. I love the mongrelness of English.

INT: I notice that the quartet which begins with *The Virgin in the Garden* is sometimes called *The Frederica Quartet*.

ASB: My paperback publisher, you will be glad to hear, is going to make it a boxed set, and it's just going to be called *The Quartet*. It isn't Frederica's book – though she's the sort of person who would muscle in and try to take it! I should never, in a way, have killed Stephanie. I only worked out about three years ago – and I don't think I shall say much more about this – that all the people I kill are myself. If people die in my books I think on the whole it's better I kill myself. Stephanie is the nearest to me. I killed the elder sister in *The Game* as well.

INT: We don't expect Stephanie to die. It's like the death of Gerald in E. M. Forster's *The Longest Journey*, where Chapter 5 begins, 'Gerald died that afternoon.'

ASB: That was one of my inspirations; and in a novel by Monica Dickens the whole of the first chapter is devoted to a pregnant woman putting the kettle on and waiting for her husband to come home: then the kettle explodes and kills her. Her husband is called Daniel, the name I gave my character. When I met Monica Dickens I told her I'd done this as a homage, not a theft, which she said was absolutely fine. These are the two deepest thoughts I have about the art of the novel. The first is the thought about metaphor and why you get excited about two being one, and the second is about chance and order. All the way through his novels Balzac says, 'chance which is order', 'chance which is fate'. If you can feel the novelist predicting a death, saying, 'This character is doomed never to live', you haven't got a representation of life. Few of us, if we're not born with a debilitating disease, are born to die, and yet we're all born to die. I wanted to put death in a novel.

I also wanted to disprove D. H. Lawrence, who said in *Women in Love* that nothing is accidental. I wanted, on the one hand, to prove that fate is fate from the moment it's happened, and, on the other, to prove that there really are accidents. It was very unfortunate that my son got killed in an accident, because it didn't feel like an accident, it felt like something I had caused by thinking about it. It was far too bad for that sort of thing to matter much, but it didn't help, exactly.

Stephanie has a life wish. The accident through which she died: that accident happened to me. The bird was quivering under the fridge, and I had two small children sleeping upstairs, and I did think, 'Help, I'm being electrocuted – what will happen to them?' I didn't bother about myself at all. That gave me an idea of what to do with Stephanie, who was brooding about what would happen to everybody else.

INT: The bird in the novel flies out of the room afterwards. Was that true as well?

ASB: Oh, yes! The only thing I couldn't get in was that our window was under the altar wall of Durham Cathedral, and it was midnight. Buried in Durham Cathedral is the Venerable Bede, who made a bird flying through a lighted hall and into the night an image of life's brevity.

INT: You wrote in one of your essays that you take random events and make them significant.

ASB: It was around the time I wrote the stories in *Sugar* – a book nobody talks about much but which was immensely important to my development as a writer – that I began to see, partly because I was stopping teaching, that *everything* can be made into a story. My ex-husband had the theory that it was to do with the death of both my parents. From then on the only person who had any expectations about what I might do was me, which was in a way a liberation. A lot of the stories in *Sugar* are for them, but they weren't going to read them. The title story was rather like that of the bird. It presented itself because of my finding – aha! – the metaphor of the sugar.

When my father was dying I talked to him about his father and realised that all that family was vanishing with him. I remembered my grandfather cooking the sugar and catching the air in the glass and making the twist of the dark and the white, and realised that the twist was a perfect metaphor for my mother always telling lies and my father always telling the truth, and both of them telling the right story, in a way. I had to write it because I'd found the right metaphor. I don't like autobiography, and didn't want to write it, but the shape required it, rather like the shape of the bird story required it. It's neither discovering nor creating an order; it's in between, and neither verb will do.

INT: You call yourself a realist writer, albeit a self-conscious one, and have said that the realist novel allows its characters to be thinking people as well as feeling people.

ASB: When I first started thinking about that, what was exciting the world I lived in were the French *nouveau roman* and critics like Gabriel Jospovici saying, very loudly and very frequently and very elegantly, that realism was dead. I remember being moved in the sixties when Frank Kermode said that we still haven't come to grips with the innovations of Forster and Lawrence. It struck me that for writers there are all sorts of beautiful things in Forster and Lawrence, in their pacing, in the way they could move from an idea to an action to a sensation to a thought.

You can't do that anywhere near as easily if you are Robbe-Grillet. You are writing much more on one note. Rereading Balzac recently, I saw things which even Proust's method has rather ironed out and stopped you from being able to do. There's loss as well as gain. Balzac is making an image of the cosmos in the shape of Paris, and it's the human comedy in the shape of the divine comedy. He's really thinking big.

INT: You are not afraid of using an omniscient narrator.

ASB: Some of my best teaching experiences were with *Middlemarch* and also with Dostoevsky, who uses a completely different omniscient narrator to George Eliot's, because he plays with it as though it's a wonderful orchestra. Sometimes his omniscient narrator is inside people's heads and sometimes it is above, uttering judgements about the nature of the universe. The novel I'm obsessed with at the moment is Dostoevsky's *The Demons* or *The Possessed*, however we translate it, which sometimes is just the gossip from the town, which is very much what George Eliot does. I get angry with critics who say that Eliot was using the God's eye view because she was very dignified and thought she was God. She didn't. It was just that she wanted to say whatever she knew in whatever was the best style to say it in. She orchestrated the styles.

I used to ask students to look at the times she uses the first-person plural: 'we all feel this'. She does this to make a statement about a universal trait. Sometimes she says, 'You may think . . . ' and she is actually addressing somebody she's not sure she agrees with. Sometimes she says, 'he thought', and sometimes she almost suggests that she doesn't quite know what somebody thought, but that it was a bit like this. She can do all those things, because she's got a flexible instrument. If you choose a first-person narrative you've thrown away every single one of those opportunities; but you may have an intensity that she doesn't have.

When I was a student at Cambridge under Dr Leavis, he was very proud of himself and sure that he was right and everybody else was wrong; but he was also sure that the writers were more right than he was; whereas now a perfectly legitimate attempt to question the authority of the text has skidded into a feeling that the text has no authority and its author doesn't understand anything. In which case you may as well give up studying literature and study Acts of Parliament. Good authors have authority and I respect them.

INT: *The Virgin in the Garden* is set mainly in Yorkshire, and in other novels you often take your characters there at some point. Do you see yourself as a provincial novelist?

ASB: I find it quite hard to do the earth if it's not Yorkshire earth. I'm beginning to be able to do the Cévennes, where I live in the summer, but that's not unlike Yorkshire. I have a kind of analogical hook. I don't like the kind of novel that's a disguised travel document. I like the feeling that for one thing I say there are twenty things I could have said. I can only really do that with Yorkshire, though the next novel has to be set in Kent or Surrey or round about there, so I persuade my husband to go out and research the earth every weekend in a car, and we have a lovely time.

When I started writing novels there was a completely wrong idea that the angry young men, the Wains and Braines, were writing the novel of the provinces which had never been written. Yet we'd already had Arnold Bennett and D. H. Lawrence, who were both infinitely better novelists than any of them had any hope of being. It comes up in every generation. Now there's a particularly angry Scottish version. I feel that the Scots are rather like the women in *Possession*: they are in a position of power because they are grouped, and have a big noise going for their group. A novelist like me living in London isn't part of any group. Your world is your own world and you fight your own battles. There isn't a discussion in any paper in this country or anywhere else of the English metropolitan novelist. There will be a discussion of the English provincial novelists, and the English woman novelist, but not of the lady novelist in Putney who tries to write books as large as she can push herself into.

INT: Do you see yourself as a historical novelist?

ASB: Yes, rather to my surprise. I read historical novelists like Walter Scott and Georgette Heyer all through my youth and never wanted to write like any of them. I didn't understand until many years later that Scott was describing societal changes almost as though they were geological changes, or Darwinian changes, which is what Balzac knows he's doing. The older you get, the more you see that you not only have your own past but the past of the society which formed you – by its limitations as well as its possibilities. For example, Hitler has become history and can be studied, whereas there's a sort of dip just behind you that you can't study at all, because it's too close. The only time I'm not planning to write about is the time just before I was born, which was when my parents met each other. A lot of the young male novelists I wrote about in the essays in *On Histories and Stories* are interested in exactly that time: how their fathers were in the war; whereas I feel strongly that that's a time that I can't get at yet. Give me another ten years and I may do.

A Whistling Woman is partly a historical novel, because I had left so long between it and *Still Life*. It was written for an audience of people who were not born when the events in the novel were taking place.

INT: Surely most great British novels are historical?

ASB: We don't understand that George Eliot was writing about her childhood or her father's childhood, because we haven't enough historical imagination. There's an article that's written every time the Booker Prize is judged which asks, 'Where are the great novels about contemporary life?' I remember Malcolm Bradbury saying, 'The Berlin Wall went down six months ago. Where is the great novel about it?' The Germans are *beginning* to write great novels about it, but you can't write one straight away.

INT: There are many scenes in *A Whistling Woman* which suggest you were planning the end of the quartet from the very beginning.

ASB: I always knew who John Ottokar was, vaguely, but when I first thought of the beginning of *The Virgin in the Garden* I certainly had not invented Peacock. But there was room in the structure for that to happen. Frederica's marriage and divorce existed, though Leo didn't. I feel she has a good relationship with Leo, rather to her surprise, and that was one of the things I thought through: what would she do if she found she had a child? She wouldn't realise how much she loved him until the scene where he followed her and got hold of her and kicked her.

INT: When discussing *Possession* in *Portraits in Fiction* you say near the start that every reader will see a different Maud and that seems like a fault; but by the end you say it's a particular virtue of the novel as opposed to cinema and, presumably, radio.

ASB: I want viewers to come back to the word on the page, which has the glory of not only letting you skip, but letting you go back twenty pages to see what it was you might have missed. Your relationship with a novel is much more empowered than your relationship with a film, which is seducing you and also moves along at its speed not yours. Even when you try to pin a character down and say, 'She had three little brown spots at regular intervals on the back of her hand', nobody will see the same hand. This seems part of the inexhaustibility of the novel: everybody sees a different woman. Equally, it's glorious that we all stare at the same painting and get something different from it. But it *is* the same painting, it doesn't change, it represents unchangingness. The thing about a novel is that you or I or anybody see different Fredericas on different readings: she doesn't stay stable. Whereas once you've got Gwyneth Paltrow as Maud it's hard to get your proper Maud back.

INT: In an essay on his contemporaries Norman Mailer talks about 'the glance round the room'. When you glance round the room, which other novelists do you see?

ASB: I greatly admire Lawrence Norfolk, who is doing all sorts of things that I would never have thought of doing but seem to me to be akin to what I do in the sense that he makes huge mythical structures, and plays with levels of reality, and winds the whole culture of Europe into fantastic tales: he's an immensely ambitious writer. I like the same quality in *Ghostwritten*, the novel of a much younger writer called David Mitchell. It's a perfect example of the readable novel that nevertheless reveals more and more, a kind of international novel that hops between cultures and worlds with great confidence. Both those novelists are doing things I recognise from where I stand but are quite different from what I do. I also liked Philip Hensher's *Kitchen Venom.* He observes very well, and is a morally generous man. I don't like people who pin their characters to the page and watch them squirm. Hensher does occasionally observe people suffer and occasionally mocks them but he has a kind of generosity and a curiosity about how people are going to behave, both in his little books and his big book. Again, he's stylistically ambitious; he's imitating nineteenth-century writing and good modern writing and Persian poetry.

I like Ali Smith's *Hotel World* very much, and Helen de Witt's *The Last Samurai*: two extraordinarily inventive novels. I also like A. L. Kennedy, speaking of the theocratic Scots! One of the good things about British writing at the moment is its immense variety. There are all sorts of people doing all sorts of things and it's only journalists talking about the Booker who say we ought to be writing more about what's going on in contemporary Britain. It's only the people who are trying to fulfil that prescription who bore me. One of my daughters interviewed Zadie Smith in San Francisco and said she's very serious and very ambitious. I like that sense of energy, and very much enjoyed her first novel. Another journalistic commonplace is that all the energy is in the American novel, and the British novel hasn't got any. I don't think those journalists ever read British novels, except Martin Amis, who certainly has energy and is wonderful too. But they sit there solemnly saying everybody isn't as good as Don DeLillo. Don DeLillo is very good but we have things just as interesting and in some ways more complicated than Don DeLillo's fiction.

I once said in the British Council in Paris, 'I can name forty-two living writers in England who either have written a great novel or might write one.' Somebody said, 'All right, do it,' so I wrote them all down on a piece of paper and missed Charles Palliser in the front row, because he was sitting there – who again has interesting, strange, complicated structures. And look at Robert Irwin. His book about the Arabian Nights is wonderful; but he's written five or six novels, none of them resembling each other. *Exquisite Corpse* is a beautiful novel. It looks light and easy and has all sorts of depths. It's a study of surrealism and the nature of loss and love, and of the turning point at the beginning of the Second World War. In some countries he would be being taught as their major writer.

INT: You often write about the effect of television and computers and the World Wide Web on reading.

ASB: Television has changed our imaginative world in ways I don't quite understand because I come from the reading world and live in the television world. There are many people who don't open books. I don't, however, think everybody has to read. Dr Leavis believed that the university English department was the cultural centre of the world, and I never wanted to believe that. I thought that biologists were doing something that English Literature students had no idea about, which was actually very important; so were the philosophers and so, even, were the lawyers. But if you want to be moral, if you want to communicate, you have to use language. Novelists still do it better than anybody else, except for Wallace Stevens and Emily Dickinson.

INT: So you feel there's no such thing as a moral painting or televisual image?

ASB: If you're going to argue about how to behave, you're going to need language. You can arouse people's anguish with Oxfam pictures, but you need to say it with words so that society can think out what to do. Language remains the element in which we move, rather like air, which means it will be quite hard to kill the novel. The novel is one person talking to another person at every single level in language. I often feel that the theatre is the thing that's died, and not the novel. The theatre has been killed by film and television. It used to create the kind of emotion you got in a church when you had a service or sang a hymn. It's much more closely connected to a religion which is dying, and to a presentation of life and language that goes with religion. I can perfectly well imagine a world without the theatre, whereas I can't quite imagine a world without the novel, or film. The novel began, in a way, with agnosticism. It's an alternative story to the Bible even if sometimes it appears to be supporting the Bible. Dostoevsky will use paradigms of Christ, or his characters will stand against a wall with their arms out being crucified, but they're ordinary people in a secular world.

Select criticism

■ Books

Alfer, Alexa and Michael J. Noble, eds. *Essays on the Fiction of A. S. Byatt: Imagining the Real.* Westport, CT: Greenwood Press, 1989.

Burgass, Catherine. *A. S. Byatt's Possession: A Reader's Guide.* New York and London: Continuum, 2002.

Franken, Christien. *A. S. Byatt: Art, Authorship, Creativity.* London: Palgrave Macmillan, 2001.

Kelly, Kathleen Coyne. *A. S. Byatt.* New York: Twayne, 1996.

Todd, Richard. *A. S. Byatt.* Plymouth: Northcote House in association with The British Council, 1997.

Wallhead, Celia M. *The Old, the New and the Metaphor: A Critical Study of the Novels of A. S. Byatt.* London: Minerva, 1999.

■ Chapters in books, pamphlets and articles

Ashworth, Ann. 'Fairy Tales in A. S. Byatt's *Possession*', *Journal of Evolutionary Psychology* 15: 1–2 (Mar. 1994), pp. 93–4.

Boccardi, Mariadale. 'Biography, the Postmodern Last Frontier: Banville, Barnes, Byatt, and Unsworth' in *Arts, Littératures & Civilisations du Monde Anglophone* 11 (Oct. 2001), pp. 149–57.

Campbell, Jane. 'The Hunger of the Imagination in A. S. Byatt's *The Game*', *Critique: Studies in Contemporary Fiction* 29: 3 (Spring 1988), pp. 147–62.

Campbell, Jane. ' "The Somehow May Be Thishow": Fact, Fiction and Intertextuality in Antonia Byatt's "Precipice Encurled" ', *Studies in Short Fiction* 28: 2 (Spring 1991), pp. 115–23.

Clutterbuck, Charlotte. 'A Shared Depositary of Wisdom: Connection and Redemption in Tiger and the Tiger Pit and *Possession*', *Southerly* 53: 2 (June 1993), pp. 121–9.

Creighton, Joanne V. 'Sisterly Symbiosis: Margaret Drabble's *The Waterfall* and A. S. Byatt's *The Game*', *Mosaic: A Journal for the Interdisciplinary Study of Literature* 20: 1 (Winter 1987), pp. 15–29.

Dusinberre, Juliet. 'Forms of Reality in A. S. Byatt's *The Virgin in the Garden*', *Critique: Studies in Contemporary Fiction* 24: 1 (Fall 1982), pp. 55–62.

Gitzen, Julian. 'A. S. Byatt's Self-Mirroring Art', *Critique: Studies in Contemporary Fiction* 36: 2 (Winter 1995), pp. 83–95.

Holmes, Frederick M. 'The Historical Imagination and the Victorian Past: A. S. Byatt's *Possession*', *English Studies in Canada* 20: 3 (Sept. 1994), pp. 319–34.

Hope, Christopher. *Contemporary Writers: A. S. Byatt.* London: The Book Trust and the British Council, 1990.

Hulbert, Ann. 'The Great Ventriloquist: A. S. Byatt's *Possession: A Romance*', in *Contemporary British Women Writers: Texts and Strategies.* London: Macmillan, 1993, pp. 55–65.

Sabine, Maureen. ' "Thou Art the Best of Mee": A. S. Byatt's *Possession* and the Literary *Possession* of Donne', *John Donne Journal: Studies in the Age of Donne* 14 (1995), pp. 127–48.

Sanchez, Victoria. 'A. S. Byatt's *Possession*: A Fairytale Romance', *Southern Folklore* 52:1 (1995), pp. 32–52.

Shiller, Dana. 'The Redemptive Past in the Neo Victorian Novel', *Studies in the Novel* 29: 4 (Winter 1997), pp. 538–60.

Todd, Richard. 'The Retrieval of Unheard Voices in British Postmodernist Fiction: A. S. Byatt and Marina Warner', in Theo D'haen and Hans Bertens, eds, *Liminal Postmodernisms: The Postmodern, the (Post-)Colonial, and the (Post-)Feminist.* Amsterdam: Rodopi, 1994, pp. 99–114.

Yelin, Louise. 'Cultural Cartography: A. S. Byatt's *Possession* and the Politics of Victorian Studies', *Victorian Newsletter* 81 (Spring 1992), pp. 38–41.

Roddy Doyle

Pat Wheeler and Jenny Newman

Roddy Doyle is the eclectic writer of novels, plays, screenplays and children's books. His early novels, *The Commitments* (1987), *The Snapper* (1990) and *The Van* (1991), are unsentimental narratives of working-class family life, set in and around his native Dublin. These novels – written in the rhythms and cadences of a colloquial Dublin 'demotic' – are frequently rude and often hilarious, and Doyle is not afraid to tackle controversial subject matter such as poverty, domestic violence and single motherhood.

Doyle sees his novels as coming from 'what he sees and what he feels'. In *Paddy Clarke Ha Ha Ha* (1993), a brutally sad and comic novel, he moves to a more introspective, first-person narrative. The novel, written entirely from the perspective of a 10-year-old boy, effectively portrays his chaotic thought patterns as he watches the breakdown of his parents' marriage. *The Woman Who Walked Into Doors* (1996) takes the domestic violence of *Paddy Clarke* a stage further and is perhaps his most controversial work. He received a great deal of criticism but remains unrepentant, claiming that 'I'm not a branch of the tourist industry and I don't see it as my job to present an idealistic vision of Ireland, or Irish families.' Doyle says he has 'always been a slave to realism' and that he has always tried to make sure that everything said and done in his novels could in fact happen. In *A Star Called Henry* (1999) he departs from his usual format. Henry Smart introduces himself from his mother's womb, mythical and legendary figures (Padraig Pearse and Michel Collins) are juxtaposed, and a convincing tale of Irish history is held together by more than a touch of magic realism.

The Commitments (director Alan Parker 1991), *The Snapper* (director Stephen Frears 1993) and *The Van* (director Stephen Frears 1997) have all been adapted for film. *The Commitments* (adapted by Doyle with Dick Clement and Ian La Frenais) received the British Academy of Film and TV Arts Best Adapted Screenplay award in 1991. Also in 1991 *The Van* was shortlisted for the Booker Prize, and in 1993 *Paddy Clarke Ha Ha Ha* was the winner of the Booker Prize. Doyle remains one of Ireland's most popular and critically acclaimed authors, a foremost chronicler of working-class lives.

Key works

■ Novels

The Commitments. London: Secker & Warburg, 1987 (orig. pub. in Dublin by
  King Farouk).
The Snapper. London: Secker & Warburg, 1990.
The Van. London: Secker & Warburg, 1991.
The Barrytown Trilogy. London: Secker & Warburg, 1992 (*The Commitments*, *The
  Snapper* and *The Van* in a single-volume edition).
Paddy Clarke, Ha Ha Ha. London: Secker & Warburg, 1993.
The Woman Who Walked Into Doors. London: Secker & Warburg, 1996.
A Star Called Henry. London: Secker & Warburg, 1999.
Rory and Ita. London: Secker & Warburg, 2002.

■ Screenplays

The Commitments (dir. Alan Parker 1991), written by Dick Clement, Ian La
  Frenais, Roddy Doyle.
The Snapper (dir. Stephen Frears 1993).
The Van (dir. Stephen Frears 1997).
When Brendan Met Trudy (dir. Kieron Walsh 2001). Original screenplay.

INT: You draw on a particular oral tradition in your writing, and your
    books have been described as full of 'hilarious slang, colloquialisms,
    vulgarisms and cursing that is so vibrant and charged it is almost
    musical'. How would you describe your use of language?

RD: I remember one of the critics said that my work had too much
    dialogue and yet the very same reviewer praised a novel by Manuel
    Puig, who writes nothing but dialogue. The comment both baffled and
    amused me. I was really happy with the language in *The Commitments*
    because it is the language I am familiar with and the language I enjoy.
    I have always enjoyed the creativity of slang and I use it myself and
    invented it a bit when I was a kid. Later on when I was teaching I
    loved leaving aside what you would call vulgarisms. When I was
    writing *The Commitments* I had a huge great gang of characters on the
    crest of adulthood who were creative in their use of language. *The Van*
    and *The Snapper* were of that same world and I felt I was on quite solid
    ground when I was writing them. I knew how the characters would
    speak because I speak like that and friends of mine speak in the same
    way. The decision to write a book about a gang of working-class kids

forming a band brought with it its own language and I was happy being stuck with it.

INT: Environment seems important to you in that it shapes and defines your characters. Do they ever transcend the social forces that shape them?

RD: A very good story usually has universal qualities, but at the same time it is normally located, from my point of view, in a square mile of that universe. So when the two things meet, as in *The Commitments*, it's a universal story. It's a dream of kids all over the world to form a band, and yet I located it within a couple of square miles of North Dublin and that made the characters human beings rather than vague humanoids. My affection for Dublin is unbounded, I like the people, I like what I hear, and in the early books I tried to capture the way I heard people talking. It was engrossing and it was fun and I also felt to an extent that theirs was a voice that really hadn't been heard much in literature. I wasn't trying to fill the hole consciously but there was a hole there so for various reasons the early books are strongly rooted in what is a fictional Dublin, but in fact is my patch of it. I'm not altogether certain why I've decided to write beyond Dublin or why, particularly, I reach out to parts of the United States such as New York and Chicago. The majority of people who left Ireland in the twenties headed west so maybe I'm following them. I grew up listening to American music and watching American movies and there are films like *The Grapes of Wrath* that are branded in my head. It's nice to create characters that walk the streets of New York or Chicago and later go into the wide-open spaces that I've been looking at and imagining all my life.

What I tried to do with *The Commitments* was to show people who are economically and culturally trapped, but rather than lie down and wallow in it, they celebrate, they scream and roar and create music about it and turn the experience into a positive thing. *The Commitments* is a very funny novel, but it also makes a serious point about the need for dignity and self-respect. If 'soul' is about escapism and revolution (as one character says), then music must be the politics of the people – the plebian voice raised in protest. Country music, the Blues and Irish traditional music are heralds of anguish, they're a cry of celebration. Music is one of the few ways that working-class people can escape.

Henry Smart in *A Star Called Henry* hopes he is making his escape. In a way he has been instrumental in finding what being Irish means because he is located in a particular time and place. He's a wanted man so he has to get out of Ireland and he wants to get as far away as he possibly can. The further he goes the more he realises that it can't be done. He arrives in New York thinking it's a new world but in fact it's a collection of European villages and he is way too late to find anything new in the place at all. So he has to keep going further. He also finds really that New York is not just Irish, but Latvian, Jewish, Italian; it's made up of little parishes and he's looking for a patch where he can reinvent himself, where he can be baptised in a way and say, 'I could start again, I'm American.' There is a geographical escape to an extent but it isn't always enough.

INT: Character is arguably the most important single component in your novels, with plot taking an almost subsidiary role in your early writing. What were your intentions in the Barrytown trilogy – a straightforward plot, but interesting characters to drive the action?

RD: Yes, that's right, the plot is very simple: kids form a band, the band gets up and running, the band breaks up, a young woman finds herself pregnant, the pregnancy, the birth. It all takes place over about nine months and that's deliberate, too. Most of the books I have loved are about people and if a so-called 'novel of ideas' (I really dislike that phrase) does not have interesting people in it then as far as I'm concerned it's not worth reading. I love W. G. Sebald's *Austerlitz*, which is full of ideas; but the narrator himself is fascinating, and the man he is writing about is even more fascinating. For me character is vital.

INT: Some critics responded adversely to Jimmy Rabbitte Jnr in *The Commitments* saying that 'the Irish are the niggers o' Europe', that 'Dubliners are the niggers o' Ireland' and the 'northside Dubliners are the niggers o' Dublin'. What does it all mean?

RD: In one way it's a joke and in another it's all about Jimmy trying to motivate his band: he is trying to instil some sort of purpose in them. It's about overcoming the legacy of colonisation and it's also there to shock people out of their respectable, middle-class positions. I was listening to a hip-hop record that my wife gave me for Christmas about a gang called the Woo Tang Gang. I played it while I was working and the word 'nigger' was coming at me all the time. What's interesting now is that every time I write the word (and it is quite a lot at the moment because I am writing about race relations and the absence of them in the 1920s), the spell check tells me that it doesn't exist. In the film script of *The Commitments* the word was taken out and the word 'black' replaced it. Alan Parker said you just couldn't get away with a white person saying 'nigger'. I thought it was a pity because it just isn't the same, and "black" doesn't have the same history. A black American guy I spoke to later said that it was a mistake. He had read the book and seen the film and thought that it should have stayed.

INT: You have talked about hearing the rhythm of the novels of, for instance, James Kelman and Salman Rushdie. Clearly rhythm plays an important part both in your writing and in your many references to music. Is the tension between the oral and the aural in your own writing deliberate or is it just the way your interests and influences come to the fore?

RD: It's both. Adding a 'soundtrack' to a book gives it an extra dimension. 'My Eyes Adored You' in *The Woman Who Walked Into Doors* is a dreadful song and yet I think it works really well on paper. People who recognise the song hear its ironies and it doesn't seem to matter to those who don't. Song lyrics work on different levels: for example, the naming of songs in *The Woman Who Walked Into Doors* allowed me to place Paula's reminiscences in a decade or a specific time in that decade. The music plays an important role in her life and at one stage she says that she doesn't know any songs from the 1980s. It was in the 1980s that she 'walked into doors' and 'picked herself up from the floor' and realised her life was unravelling. In *The Commitments* the change in the lyrics from either Chicago or Detroit or Memphis to Dublin hammered home my point. It was great fun to do and far more entertaining than writing a paragraph explaining the context.

I tend to listen to music as I work. When I gave up teaching and found myself with the whole day to write, I thought it was an opportunity to listen to new music. I'm listening to a lot of jazz at the moment as research for my book but I am also listening to music that says something about the rhythm that I want to capture. There's a piece called 'Different Trains' by Steve Reich that's got great rhythm and has speaking voices on a loop. The history of the piece is fascinating. When Reich was very young his parents divorced and shared custody; one lived in New York and the other in Los Angeles and twice a year Reich crossed America on a train, with his nanny, I think. He recorded her talking about the journey and took snippets of what she was saying about the trains and then recorded a black train porter talking. He has a combination of driving music and the repetition of voices and the places that they passed through. Reich's childhood coincided with the holocaust so while he was going back and forth across America, in Europe Jews were travelling on trains to the concentration camps. The middle part of 'Different Trains' is about this. There's something about the repetition and the chaos and narrative running through it that I love, and in some ways I am trying to capture this in the book I am writing at the moment. So it's not just words, it's the rhythm of those words as well. A Belgian company recently produced an opera of *The Woman Who Walked Into Doors* and I went to Antwerp to watch it. What startled me (there are two women on stage, one speaking and the other singing) was that not only were the spoken words directly from *The Woman Who Walked Into Doors,* but so were the lyrics. They weren't quite *songs* as I would understand them, just lines or sentences from the novel, not even trimmed or pruned. It was quite extraordinary to hear.

INT: I'm not surprised actually because there is a musical cadence and rhythm to your writing.

RD: It is probably more apparent in the recent books which have more description than the earlier books; I am quite happy to sacrifice reality for a good rhythm. I just won't let go of a sentence unless I feel that it flows and spend an awful lot of time on making sure that every sentence I write has that certain rhythm. If a word has an extra syllable I ditch it and put one in that probably swings the story in a slight direction I didn't intend – but the rhythm stays intact.

INT: Do you see a substantial difference between the Irish novel and the English novel?

RD: I think there is something to be said about English being the more recent language to us, but the Irish is bubbling away there under the surface. Our stories are automatically different because we grew up differently. In the twentieth century, particularly, a new definition of Irishness was forced upon people who had never given it a second thought and suddenly we were consciously Irish. I think there is creativity or a certain flair to Irish writing but it would be wrong to look at every Irish writer and say that this is true. There is a flair, which is not necessarily a complimentary thing, but there is flair and music to the language that perhaps isn't there in English despite its other strengths. The knocking of the English novel gets on my wick, you know. It has had a bad press from people who should know better. There are a lot of sweeping generalisations which don't mean an awful lot.

INT: How do you feel about the labels that have been attached to you and your work? Do you see yourself as representing Irish literature?

RD: I shy away from that type of thing. Sometimes one reads or hears that one is supposed to be representing Irish writing but I don't see myself as representing anybody except myself. I am quite happily and cheerfully Irish most of the time. At the moment I am writing about Chicago, but very much from an Irishman's perspective in the early twenty-first century. I don't see myself as a self-consciously Irish writer. I never have done and I hope never to see myself in that way and I don't see any schools of writing in Ireland at the moment. I do see some very good writing and some pretty poor writing but I don't see any schools or groups or unity. I'm not sure what the Irish literary tradition *is*. I'm Irish and I'm a writer and I'm definitely influenced by the place and the language.

INT: Are your novels received differently away from Ireland?

RD: *The Van* is probably the most obvious case in point. A bad review in Britain and America was a rare thing. The reviews were very enthusiastic and it was shortlisted for the Booker Prize. In Ireland it only got one good review. All the others were very dismissive, extraordinarily dismissive. To say there was a difference in the way I was received is to put it mildly.

INT: What was the objection to *The Van*?

RD: It was primarily the language. One reviewer actually counted the number of times the word 'fuck' appeared, which is more than I did. There were objections to what were seen as stereotypical depictions of working-class people. But once I began to get a bit of recognition beyond Ireland – when *The Van* was shortlisted for the Booker Prize – suddenly people started changing their minds, which was quite amusing to watch. I think that hostility has died somewhat although there is a certain amount still evident. On the other hand, I had a film released last year, a romantic comedy called *When Brendan Met Trudy*, and the reviews in Ireland were terrific. I think they 'got' it and really enjoyed it whereas the reviews from Britain were very dismissive and in some instances I thought they were racist, which really surprised me. The difference in response is really quite interesting.

INT: Does that make you think about your potential readership when you embark on a writing project?

RD: I don't know who my potential readers are or who my actual readers are. I don't think there is such a thing as a typical reader. I'm not aware that there's any particular group of people either in terms of age or gender or nationality who read my books. I want clarity in my writing and there are a lot of phrases that are very Irish but I would never go out of my way to explain them. It would be bad writing. You have to hope that they go with it. Clarity and explanation are two different things, and I would hate to dilute what I write so that someone in Milwaukee can 'get' it. At the moment I'm beginning to get a little anxious because I am writing about black characters and I want to make sure I get it right. I let the rhythm dictate how the characters speak in a lot of cases but I would hate to get it hugely wrong. That's more to do with me and my wish to produce a piece of work that's good rather than thinking in terms of an African American readership which may not exist for my work.

INT: You have moved from a proliferation of dialogue and third-person narratives in your early work to first-person narration in *Paddy Clark Ha Ha Ha* and *The Woman Who Walked Into Doors* and a more omniscient narrator in *A Star Called Henry*. Is this a deliberate shift?

RD: In *The Commitments* the decision to write about a band brought the dialogue with it. There were lots of working-class kids queuing up to be heard in that book and the shape reflects that. After that I decided to write something in the same vein but more intimate, and once again the setting dictated the narrative. *The Van* and *The Snapper* are set in houses full of people all talking at once, or in pubs full of people all wanting to talk. These people are talking, talking, talking, and I just love a burst of dialogue.

When I finished the Barrytown trilogy I thought, well that's that, and didn't see any need for another book in that vein. There are various reasons why I chose to write in the first person, but I did it mainly because I thought rather than being the reader's guide I would *be* that person. First-person narration dictates the inward nature of the narrative. I enjoyed using it and I thought it worked very well so I decided to use it in *The Woman Who Walked Into Doors*.

I would like to write something short in the third person but I can't for a while. I'm kind of stuck with the first person because I am writing a big story that is going to take me years. Henry is alone quite a lot of the time and I just get him into a diner so he can start talking to somebody. It's Prohibition so he can't just walk into a pub: he has to go somewhere and find out the secret knock and hope that he gets in. I try to define my characters through dialogue even though they may speak with the same accent. They all have a particular way of expressing themselves. There may be a couple of words they use which aren't generally used by others or there's a hesitation in the way they speak. I try to give them their stamp by the way they talk rather than their physical description.

INT: Why did you choose to use long dashes rather than speech marks in much of your writing?

RD: I thought the dashes (for which I am sometimes ludicrously criticised) were more immediate than the formality of the speech marks. When I began to write the first book, I wrote it longhand and then typed it. I don't remember whether I used the speech marks in longhand or the dashes but I do know when I started experimenting with typing, a dash was much quicker. I liked its appearance on the page and it reminded me of Flann O'Brien, who I read when I was a teenager. There were occasions when he didn't use speech marks at all in his writing and I loved that welding of the dialogue to the narrative. In my current book I have abandoned speech marks. I use italics now and again although I don't like their appearance; but I do think they're useful and I'll use either a syllable or a word in italics, and now and again a shout conveyed in capitals or even bold. Sometimes just writing a sentence by itself doesn't quite capture the way you want that sentence to be heard.

INT: Richard Hoggart acknowledges that 'to write of a working-class mother is to run peculiar risks', and he believes her place in many representations of working-class life is either 'honoured' or 'careless'. Do you feel that his views are relevant to your representation of Veronica in *The Snapper* and of women in general?

RD: I write about the working classes so, of course, working-class mothers play an important role. I suppose in some ways working-class mothers try to keep everything going, and Veronica is typical in that respect. She is a bit of a martyr where the children are concerned and some of the humour comes out of that. I wanted to show how different aspects of life impact on the family. The kids want to take up ballroom dancing so the mother provides the means for them to do it. She makes the clothes and sews the sequins. Of course by the time she's done that they've moved on to the next thing. I wanted to show something of the throwaway culture that invades their lives, to show how things change and how mothers attempt to keep up in whatever way they can. Women are important in *The Snapper* and *The Van*, not just as mothers. They're sexual beings and they talk about men in the same way men talk about women. Men talk about football and sex and the women talk about men and sex. They're rowdy and bawdy and very funny. Sharon is an important character, and I suppose it was quite a political move on my part to have a young, unmarried woman as the focus of attention. She is not hidden away as she might have been but accepted by the family.

INT: *Paddy Clarke Ha Ha Ha* never diverges for a second from the viewpoint of a small boy and everything appears to flow from his train of thought. Yet the novel also describes a failing marriage, domestic violence, religion, sex, growing up, and not least the changing face of Barrytown itself. You use first-person narrative, interior monologue and you juxtapose thoughts, memories, personal information, facts gleaned from books, stories, parables – a never-ending variety of narratives. How did you get all the little episodes to fit together and flow?

RD: *Paddy Clarke Ha Ha Ha* took me a very long time to write and initially it was hard going. I'd decided I wanted to write about a boy watching his parents' marriage break up. I wanted to capture his chaotic thought patterns and that was difficult to do. First-person narrative is ideal for this sort of interiority of thought but I did have some difficulty with continuity and connection and with the incorporation of some of my ideas about the narrative. I wrote and rewrote sections and moved them around until I had what I wanted. But of course our minds are made up of a jumble of thoughts, memories, snatches of songs – almost everything we see and read is there somewhere. That's always difficult to get down on paper and even more so in the voice of a ten-year-old. I had to try to remember what it was like to be ten years old and while I was writing memories came back to me gradually, in bits and pieces, and I incorporated some of them into the book. So you could say that the inspiration for the novel came from my own life, although it is fiction. My parents are still together, for example, but I mixed all sorts of memories of my childhood. I found a book in my parents' attic about Father Damien and the lepers which I thought was wonderful and so I decided that was going to be Paddy's favourite book.

INT: Why did you footnote the Irish phrases?

RD: In Ireland very few people speak Irish even though they did it every day between five to eighteen. It was and still is a compulsory subject at primary and secondary levels, and things like 'May I have permission to go to the toilet?' and vital stuff like that are all part of Paddy's ten-year-old world. The translations are for the benefit of readers. I don't like it when I turn a page and there's a passage in German or French or Greek or Hebrew. There's something very pompous and just stupid about not giving the people the benefit of translation.

INT: The novel is both very funny and brutally sad. The football commentary by the young lad is pitch perfect and the rules and intricacies of shoplifting are wonderfully realised. Yet the scene where Paddy first realises his father hits his mother, the spare, fragmented writing – 'I walked. I listened. I stayed in. I guarded' – really evokes his fear. How hard was it to get into the mind of a ten-year-old boy dealing with these issues?

RD: I was trying to capture the world of a ten-year-old kid when sometimes that world is hilariously funny and sometimes it can be very violent and very frightening. I thought about myself when I was that age and the things I remembered most were the freedom but also the fear. I also remember using humour as a sort of tool against people I didn't like and so I saw all these aspects of the boy's life as integral. Paddy's friends let him down and his father lies to him. There is certainly a feeling of loss at the end of the novel but there is also hope. Paddy finds out about the realities of the wider world at a very young age and he has to grow up fairly quickly. But what he feels in the novel – the freedom, the fear and the cruelty – are all part of the process. He has to confront these things in order to leave them behind.

INT: You have described *The Woman Who Walked Into Doors* as 'the most difficult thing I've ever written'. How did you turn yourself from the man who wrote the Barrytown trilogy and *Paddy Clarke* into the man who wrote this novel?

RD: The background to the novel comes from a character in a series I wrote for television called *Family*, the last of which is told from the wife's point of view. When I was writing the fourth and final episode I thought I could take the character of the wife further. I wanted to get to know the character of Paula really well and I felt she had a lot more to say. I wanted to show why she had married Charlo and why she had stayed with him when he was so violent. The heaviest criticism I've ever received was about the domestic violence in *Family* and *The Woman Who Walked Into Doors*. There was huge public denunciation from all sorts of people, including politicians and priests, who said I seemed to be undermining the sanctity of marriage, which, of course, was exactly what I was doing. It was as if no wives or children had ever been the subject of domestic violence, and the sanctity of the family had to be kept at all cost. It was said that I'd compromised family values and misrepresented Irish life – and that violence didn't exist in Catholic households. That made me laugh. Family values are puritanical ideas that people bandy about – just right-wing nonsense. I'm not a branch of the tourist industry and I don't see it as my job to present an idealistic vision of Ireland, or Irish families. I can take criticism easily and it doesn't bother me that much. Ireland is much more open now and they're beginning to pass legislation on the issue of domestic violence.

INT: Why did you use the first person again in *The Woman Who Walked Into Doors*?

RD: I had to do a lot of research and I had to find the right tone of narrative voice. I wrote *Paddy Clarke Ha Ha Ha* in the first person to see if I could do something different, and I used it again because I thought it would be a much more powerful book if told from the point of view of the person on the receiving end of the violence. I didn't want to use a third-person narrator as I thought it would distance the reader. It was important to me that I explore Paula's life. It was also a sort of exercise to try to use the voice of a thirty-nine-year-old woman. I try to get over a character through the use of dialogue and I tried to get close to Paula's experience by using parts of my own life. Not that I've ever been an alcoholic or been close to domestic violence of any kind, but some of the childhood and teenage experiences are shared histories. It took me about two years to write and I was very happy with the book when I'd finished.

INT: Paula's refrain throughout is, 'Ask me. Ask me. Ask me.' She exists in a nightmare that does not end even when Charlo is dead. She is convinced that if her memories of a happy childhood can be confirmed she can make sense of her life. Why is that so important?

RD: Paula speaks in a flat, hesitant tone and that's deliberate; but inside she is crying out for help. She is the type of character who is never going to make a huge success of her life in terms of upward mobility. She cleans offices for companies and houses for middle-class housewives – that's what she does, nothing more and nothing less – and she drinks. The book is about Paula trying to make sense of her life. What she does is look back on her life and try to reconcile what she remembers with what her sister remembers – and, of course, it doesn't match up. She's an alcoholic, and it's very hard for a woman alcoholic; she's been through a very violent marriage that she has had the courage to try to get away from and so she has to try to separate what she *thinks* happened in her life from what *actually* happened. She is a very resilient person and a great survivor but her scars will always be with her. I wanted to shape Paula's life so that there was no beginning, middle or end to her relationship with Charlo. The narrative reflects that there is no way out of the violence for Paula even when Charlo is dead.

INT: *A Star Called Henry* is a historical novel with a central character born at the beginning of the century. Did you see this as a potential problem?

RD: It was extremely difficult to find my way into the novel and initially I couldn't get started at all. I found I didn't know enough about the history of Ireland and I had to research those times to fill in the gaps. In *A Star Called Henry* the character came first and the history followed along afterwards. The narrator, Henry, was born in Dublin at the beginning of the twentieth century and so he grew up in turbulent and violent times. This is reflected in the novel.

I wanted to see if I could write a story along the same lines as *David Copperfield* or *Nicholas Nickleby* that starts at the beginning and follows a life through to the end. I also wanted to look at different traditions of writing and to try out a bit of magic realism. I wanted to do something different. I wanted to show the degradation and abjection of the poverty and for readers to see what drove many ordinary working-class men and women to join the revolution. I researched the social and political history through books, memoirs and newspaper reports. I've said this before but when I was reading the descriptions of 1916 I thought there was a surreal quality to what was happening and I hope this is reflected in the novel. They were extraordinary times and that is what I hoped to capture. The story has taken on a life of its own – it just got longer and longer – and so I plan to take Henry's story further.

INT: You've talked in the past about which writers influence you: Joyce Carol Oates's use of repetition, for example, which influenced *Paddy Clarke Ha Ha Ha*, and Dickens's use of poverty, which helped inspire parts of *A Star Called Henry*. Are these major influences?

RD: I read a lot for research purposes and every book I've ever read has influenced me. For example, Doris Lessing's *A Proper Marriage* was a great influence on *The Snapper* and *Black Water* by Joyce Carol Oates came back into my mind when I was writing *The Woman Who Walked Into Doors*. Richard Ford's *Wildlife* influenced *Paddy Clarke Ha Ha Ha* to an extent; but I read all the time so different books influence me at different times. I'm writing a novel that's set in the United States in the twenties so I recently reread Upton Sinclair's *The Jungle*. It's packed with the detail of the time and it describes the geography of Chicago that I need for the new book. Allan Spear's *Black Chicago: The Making of a Negro Ghetto 1890–1920* is really interesting in this context and well written. I also admire W. G. Sebald and find his work profoundly moving and brilliantly written. I've bought a whole raft of biographies either written or ghostwritten by musicians such as Louis Armstrong, Duke Ellington, Paul Robeson and Hoagie Carmichael.

INT: Do you see yourself as a political writer?

RD: I suppose I do see myself as a political writer although not always in the ways that many might see. When you write about working-class life and have working-class characters then you can't help but be political. *The Woman Who Walked Into Doors* is probably the most political of my novels, but *The Snapper, The Van* and *The Commitments* are all important in giving working-class people a voice and a vibrancy of life that's often missing in literary representation. *A Star Called Henry* is political in that it is set at a key time in Irish history. My writing is about many things and politics is an integral part of it.

INT: There are certain places and characters that reappear in your work and you do tend to leave characters at particular points in the narrative. Is this always a conscious decision and are you, as your readers might be, interested in seeing what has become of them and how they have developed or moved on? Will you for example revisit Barrytown at any stage?

RD: There's a monthly free newspaper here in Dublin that two Nigerian journalists founded called *Metro* that is quite a successful attempt at a multicultural paper. I have been writing an episodic short story for them (although it's not short any more as it's actually approaching multivolume length) at the rate of a chapter a month. It's a mock sequel to *The Commitments* which is called *The Deportees*. Jimmy Rabbitte, now a middle-aged man with a bunch of kids, has a last stab at band management and forms a multiracial band. What I am trying to do there is get them to talk and if I look back over it, as it stands the few Irish people in the band are doing the bulk of the talking. I think maybe the people who are on the verge of being deported anyway don't feel that secure and are reluctant to talk – that's my excuse anyway. There are one or two characters that haven't opened their mouths yet. I'm reluctant to use the name Barrytown again as it became a dreadful cliché for a while and any working-class area in Dublin with a problem was branded Barrytown. I have enjoyed writing the story as I like writing about Dublin in the present day. If nothing else I have done the research. I couldn't see myself sitting down to write another novel about the Rabbitte family, but who knows, by the time I've finished with Henry Smart it might be something I would run to.

INT: What interests you in the contemporary novel?

RD: Nothing in particular interests me in the contemporary novel, other than the writing. I admire the work of Anne Tyler, Joyce Carol Oates, Dermot Healy, Richard Ford. They're the names that spring to mind – today. I recently read Monica Ali's *Brick Lane*, and loved it. And DBC Pierre's *Vernon God Little* – what a book!

INT: What are you working on at the moment?

RD: I'm editing a new novel, the second part of Henry Smart's story. It will be published in September 2004. I've also just finished a new book for children, my third, *The Meanwhile Adventures*. It will also be out in September 2004 – a busy month!

Select criticism

■ Books

Pasche, Ulrike. *No Mean City?: The Image of Dublin in the Novels of Dermot Bolger, Roddy Doyle and Val Mulkems*. Frankfurt: Peter Lang, 1998.

Reynolds, Margaret and Noakes, Jonathan. *Roddy Doyle*. London: Vintage, 2004.

White, Caramine. *Reading Roddy Doyle*. Syracuse, NY: Syracuse University Press, 2001.

■ Articles

Booker, Keith. 'Late Capitalism Comes to Dublin: "American" Popular Culture in the Novels of Roddy Doyle', *ARIEL: A Review of International English Literature* 28: 3 (July 1997), pp. 27–45.

Cosgrove, Brian. 'Roddy Doyle's Backward Look: Tradition and Modernity in *Paddy Clarke Ha Ha Ha*', *Studies: An Irish Quarterly Review* 85: 339 (Autumn 1996), pp. 231–42.

Dawson, Janis. 'Aspects of the Fantastic in Roddy Doyle's *A Star Called Henry*: Deconstructing Romantic Nationalism', *Journal of the Fantastic in the Arts* 12: 2, 46 (2001), pp. 168–85.

Donnelly, Brian. 'Roddy Doyle: From Barrytown to the GPO', *Irish University Review: A Journal of Irish Studies* 30: 1 (Spring–Summer 2000), pp. 17–31.

McGlynn, Mary. ' "But I Keep on Thinking and I'll Never Come to a Tidy Ending": Roddy Doyle's Useful Nostalgia', *Lit: Literature Interpretation Theory* 10: 1 (July 1999), pp. 87–105.

Onkey, Lauren. 'Celtic Soul Brothers', *Eire-Ireland: A Journal of Irish Studies* 28: 3 (Fall 1993), pp. 147–58.

Pirroux, Lorraine. ' "I'm Black an' I'm Proud": Re-Inventing Irishness in Roddy Doyle's *The Commitments*', *College Literature* 25: 2 (Spring 1998), pp. 45–57.

Strongman, Luke. 'Toward an Irish Literary Postmodernism: Roddy Doyle's *Paddy Clarke Ha Ha Ha*', *Canadian Journal of Irish Studies* 23: 1 (July 1997), pp. 31–40.

4 Alan Hollinghurst

Pat Wheeler

Alan Hollinghurst was marked out as a writer of promise by his selection as one of the 'Best Young British Novelists' of 1993. His debut novel, *The Swimming-Pool Library* (1988), established him as a witty and commanding writer with its defiant and unapologetic gay standpoint and broke new ground in its uninhibited writing about male desire for the male body. It was a breakthrough for British gay literature – the first major 'crossover' novel from gay fiction to the mainstream. In its depiction of frequent, often violent and transitory sexual encounters it is not so much concerned with breaking the silence around gay sexuality (although clearly it does this) as with how 'the sexual element was naturally central' to the lives of the men about whom he wrote. *The Swimming-Pool Library* synthesises the strands of gay writing which Hollinghurst saw as separated into pornography and 'worthy' works of sensibility and suffering. The novel received the Somerset Maugham Award in 1988, the Lambda Literary Award for Gay Men's First Novel and the Gay/Lesbian Book Award (American Library Association) in 1989.

Hollinghurst's second novel, *The Folding Star* (1994), paints a picture of people and their private worlds. It charts a young Englishman's obsession with the seventeen-year-old Flemish boy he is tutoring and has been likened to Nabokov's *Lolita* in its lusting quest for and obsession with a younger man and its narrator's futile and often humorous attempts to glimpse sight of his 'beloved'. The novel was shortlisted for the Booker Prize in 1994 and won the James Tait Black Prize for Fiction.

Hollinghurst's novels key quite self-consciously into areas of high culture, but he is equally absorbed by notions of raw lust and sexuality. All his fictional works are steeped in literary tradition, and the influences of Romantic and Victorian poetry pervade his writing, no more so than in *The Folding Star*, with its overt (and covert) references to Milton, Wordsworth and Gerald Manley Hopkins. In *The Spell* (1998) Hollinghurst moves from the first-person narration he employed in his first two novels to a freer, more omniscient third person. This allows him to lead readers through an intricate narrative of love, lust, midsummer madness and betrayal.

Key works

■ Novels

The Swimming-Pool Library. London: Chatto & Windus, 1988.
The Folding Star. London: Chatto & Windus, 1994.
The Spell. London: Chatto & Windus, 1998.
The Line of Beauty: London: Chatto & Windus, 2004.

■ Select other writing

Isherwood is at Santa Monica. Oxford: Sycamore Press, 1975.
Confidential Chats with Boys. Oxford: Sycamore Press, 1982.
Bajazet by Racine, trans. Alan Hollinghurst. London: Chatto & Windus, 1991.
New Writing 4, ed. A. S. Byatt and Alan Hollinghurst. London: Vintage: 1995.
Three Novels by Ronald Firbank, introd. Alan Hollinghurst. Harmondsworth: Penguin, 2000.
A. E. Housman, ed. Alan Hollinghurst. London: Faber & Faber, 2001.
The Ivory Tower by Henry James, introd. Alan Hollinghurst. New York: New York Review of Books, 2004.

INT: Your fiction has been seen by some as incredibly 'highbrow', while others see it as a fine example of 'literary' writing. Do you self-consciously seek to produce writing that is underpinned by theoretical and philosophical ideas?

AH: Not at all consciously, no. I've always had quite a strong aversion to theory and came through my undergraduate and graduate life early enough to avoid having to come to terms with it. I took my second degree in 1979, so I just managed to dodge it. Of course, when I was working as an editor on the *TLS* all through the eighties a lot of theory passed across my desk, and as a result I think I picked up on theory, as on various other subjects, in a very superficial way. It has never interested me much, and I've certainly never consciously worked on building something with a theoretical underpinning. That's clearly quite a different question from that of being 'literary' or not. I suppose you could say I was unselfconsciously literary; although one never really knows how one writes until one hears it described by other people. I try to write accurately and exactly and musically, and I suspect I'm sometimes tempted into being unduly sonorous. I go through spasms of disliking the way I write. I think my style has changed over the four books I've written, and that's partly to do with what they are about. The first two books are written in the first person, which I think encourages a certain freedom or extravagance that is rarely so appropriate in a third-person narration. *The Spell* is leaner and sparer in style; *The Line of Beauty* probably different again.

INT: I am interested in the idea of the English novel as opposed to the British novel and the way writers comment on it. Blake Morrison, for example, calls *The Swimming-Pool Library* 'deeply English'. You say that Ishiguro is 'purer than most English novelists'. Can you say something about this idea?

AH: *The Swimming-Pool Library* is very obviously about English predicaments and about things in English life, both in the book's present and in looking back over the earlier part of the century. Some things about it are more English than British because it is to do with an English sense of class. Its treatment of race might be seen as more British than English. Whether Morrison meant there was something deeply English in the way it was written – I don't know. It does make conscious allusions to a particularly English history of gay writers and artists, such as Firbank, Forster and Britten. I think the idea of being 'deeply English' or British is something that becomes highlighted by contrast. You'll find that people talk about my books in the United States as being very British, sometimes as being too British, as if this somehow makes them impenetrable to someone of a different culture. Ishiguro is someone who has brought a very non-English way of seeing to bear on English subjects.

INT: Contemporary British writers are often compared (unfavourably) to American writers. Dale Peck recently argued in *The New Republic* that the majority of British novelists fail to connect, in the sense that Forster writes about connection. Peck believes the current crop of British novelists has managed to ruin the British novel. (Although he does say 'At least there is Alan Hollinghurst, who is as pleasantly proficient as Forster ever was.')

AH: A lot of criticism of the British novel is that it is provincial and navel-gazing as opposed to the omnivorous, gigantic American novel. There is some truth in that, I suppose; there seems to be more of a hunger in America than there is in Britain for books that overtly address big topics. They may prefer books that 'take things on', a consideration which doesn't in itself interest me, or, I suspect, a lot of British writers.

I think many of us prefer to go at things obliquely, by inference. Looking at what I've written, I can see that *The Swimming-Pool Library* deals with an 'issue' more than the other books do. The others are about all sorts of subjects such as art, love and desire. These are general and eternal topics rather than burningly contemporary ones. There are, of course, British writers who do that sort of thing; Pat Barker is one of them. In my experience American reviewers tend to be more earnest and moralistic than British ones, and deaf to particular British ironies and tones of voice. For example, I felt the only American review of *The Spell* that completely understood it and the way it was written was by Michael Wood in the *New York Review of Books*, and he is British. The truth is that there is so much variety in British fiction at the moment that is hard, if not pointless, to generalise about it.

INT: Salman Rushdie once remarked that 'I think, like most writers, that I am most completely myself when I write and not the rest of the time. I have a social self, and my full self can't be released except in the writing.' Other writers eschew any relationship between their writing and personal experience. Where do you place yourself in this debate?

AH: My writing is deeply about me, often in ways I don't see until a long time afterwards, and even though I've never written in any way autobiographically. When I look back I see that my books do suggest some sort of emotional and psychological history. Whether I am most myself in my books I don't know. My books are certainly very personal. I think it's often confusing for people to read novels by close friends, particularly if they are written in the first person, because they bring to them so much of their personal knowledge of the author. They have continuously to separate in their minds the person they know, the writer, from the character who is speaking. There are all sorts of things in my books that I don't see until the book is done, which is reassuring. So much effort and concentration has to be put into the co-ordination of the surface of the book and its structure that I'm often not aware of other things I am saying or doing until I talk to people about it afterwards. If I have a new book out I always find that when the first person comes to interview me about it I have almost nothing to say, because I don't really know, until people tell me, what the book is about or what it's like. I don't know what's going to strike people. I write in a very private way, and never show anything to anybody until I've finished a draft of a book about which I'm pretty confident. It's often a surprise what people say.

INT: *The Swimming-Pool Library* has been described as preoccupied with the changing relationship between same-sex love and the British establishment. This is powerfully realised by Lord Nantwich's diaries and photographs and also by Will Beckwith's personal history. Is this something you set out particularly to examine?

AH: It's not a very long novel and it doesn't have any pretensions to being a comprehensive history of gay life in Britain in the twentieth century. All you get is a bit of history through the eyes of two contrasted but related characters. I would always shy away from trying to do anything which claimed to be representative of a position or to speak for a particular body of experience. At the same time the novel touches on, or alludes to, a history of homosexuality. It spotlights moments of that history I suppose. That was planned and quite deliberate, yes. Lord Nantwich was born when Oscar Wilde died, which is not deeply significant, except insofar as I was aiming for a sense of continuity in that history. But the moments chosen from Nantwich's past to be shown in the book are mainly rather personal ones. Apart from the 1954 diary that describes his arrest, the episodes aren't specifically concerned with significant moments of gay history; they are significant episodes in the life of one gay man.

INT: Blake Morrison also describes *The Swimming-Pool Library* as 'bravely carnal' and acclaims the breaking of new ground in your uninhibited writing about male desire. It is also seen as a 'crossover' novel from gay writing to mainstream. What do you think?

AH: I didn't set out to design it like that but that is how people have written and talked about the novel, so there is some truth in it I suppose. When it was published in 1988 it came at just a moment when that seemed possible. There really hadn't been much in this country written about gay sexual behaviour in a remotely literary way, so it seemed to me this was something novel and interesting to do. I know Edmund White has said the same thing about writing his books about America. If there was literature that addressed these subjects it was either American or possibly French. I don't think there was much in Britain before *The Swimming-Pool Library*. There were pornographic things on the one hand, and on the other there were novels by very accomplished writers like Francis King which touched upon aspects of gay life. Angus Wilson produced books with gay characters, but a book unapologetically seen from a gay standpoint seemed to me to be an interesting project. I wanted to try to synthesise those strands that had become separated into pornography and suffering sensibility, and to show that the sexual element is naturally central to the lives of gay people, as it is to everybody's life, and to tell some truths about that fact. I have always thought that the way to write about sex is to treat it as seriously and describe it as beautifully and accurately as you describe everything else. You try not to belittle it by the use of clichés; you try and show its interest, which is all you can really do for anything.

INT: Will Beckwith in *The Swimming-Pool Library* calls the summer of 1983 his *belle époque* – and talks about 'the faint flicker of calamity seen out of the corner of his eye'. All four novels refer back nostalgically to a time when sexual excess and promiscuity was the norm – a sort of hankering after the past. Is *The Spell* more a book of its time in that you temper the sexual excesses?

AH: Yes, it's different in tone from the first two and that's clearly significant. I suppose it is in part a book about sexual excess and sexual experimentation, but it is much more about getting older and learning to live with changes brought by time. It's a book about change in all sorts of ways, and about how people choose to make changes in their lives, but it doesn't have so keen a nostalgia for an earlier period. Alex is the character with the most nostalgic and retrospective temperament, and is more like Edward Manners in *The Folding Star* than anyone else in the book, but he is deliberately offset by the unsentimental Danny.

INT: What was it about the 1980s that made it acceptable to write about these things?

AH: Well in the early 1980s there was a rather brief window between the changes in sexual offence laws and the beginning of AIDS, though I didn't know when I started writing *The Swimming-Pool Library* at the beginning of 1984 that that would be the case. I was simply interested in contrasting a period of freedom with earlier, more difficult periods. But of course as I wrote the book, AIDS was changing the very landscape of the present-day world I was evoking. The book's moment, the summer of 1983, took on a historical significance I hadn't previously imagined.

INT: Were you surprised at how successful the novel was, considering it was breaking new ground with controversial subject matter?

AH: I was rather, but again I hadn't, of course, anticipated the Local Government Bill and the discussion about Clause 28. In publicity terms the book actually benefited from that debate in early 1988, as it was held up as the sort of thing that might be banned from public libraries. This ensured it got noticed. My book and a gay autobiographical novel by Stephen Spender, *The Temple*, came out at almost exactly the same time, I remember, and were discussed together. But no, I hadn't expected my book to take off particularly. I had failed to sell the paperback rights before publication, which made me very gloomy about its prospects; so everything that happened after that was a lovely surprise.

INT: Edmund White writes with an ideal reader in mind and says that it used to be a woman but it is now other gay men, young and old. Do you have a particular reader in mind when you write?

AH: I don't, in fact I almost deliberately do the opposite. I try to shut out any sense of expectation, although sometimes I think a particular person may be amused by a particular joke, and I hope generally of course to please people. I don't have an idea of my readership and I'm sure I would find it inhibiting and distracting if I felt there was a particular audience that I had to please. The primary thing is to try to please myself, which sadly but inevitably I never completely do. My hope is to make the book as good as possible, to work out the problem I have set myself as perfectly as I can. Anything else is subsequent to that.

INT: Do you think women feel excluded when they come to your fiction as a body of work?

AH: People are constantly reading about worlds where they are not present. That's the wonderful thing about fiction: you read about all sorts of experiences that are not your own. That's a great force for good I think. I can distinguish two classes of women's reactions that have been reported to me. One is finding the whole thing rather remote because of a lack of female characters with whom they can identify and the lack of female interest generally in the book. The other is finding the books interesting and exciting, especially if the women reading are interested in men, because the books are about men, after all. The decisions one makes about what to read are doubtless coloured by many things, acknowledged and unacknowledged. My books are, in part at least, about sex, and readers, male or female, are drawn towards things which touch on their own fantasies. That may at least be why some women do find my books erotic.

INT: In *The Folding Star* when Edward returns to England for Dawn's funeral, there is a long section on childhood, family, the awakening of sexuality and first love. It's wonderfully evocative. In *The Swimming-Pool Library* the past is always present through Nantwich's diaries, and *The Spell* starts retrospectively with Robin looking back, briefly, to his time in the desert. I wondered how important memory is in your writing?

AH: Memory is one of the writer's main resources. It's what makes writing possible at all. It's an obvious but fundamental point, that as a writer you have wells of memories to dip into, memories which you can bring up from your own past and by extension from the past of your characters. There is a connection between the acts of memory that I perform and the acts of memory performed by the characters in the book and a lot that I write tends to be rather retrospective. What these characters are doing is akin to what one does as a writer, constructing something out of what we have seen in the world. I don't think I have any particular theories about memory and time, but I am often seduced by some avenue of memory, some chain of association, that opens up unexpectedly in the process of writing.

INT: There's also the idea of a life being lived outside or behind a facade that comes over in *The Folding Star* and in *The Spell*. In *The Spell* a character takes ecstasy and says that it gives you the feeling that you are on the inside of life rather than on the outside. In *The Folding Star* Matt and Edward are 'hidden away behind old people'. Are they on the outside or hidden away, and is your writing an attempt to bring these characters to the foreground, to the centre?

AH: I am certainly interested in what's going on behind anything that's said or done. As a writer one interprets what is being said and the shading and atmosphere in the book is an expression of all sorts of things which aren't directly expressed by the character but which richly inform you of their private lives. That's very important to me. I think that Edward has the sense of being outside some mystery, which is to do with love and sex and reciprocated desire. In *The Folding Star* there is a similar passage to the one you mention in *The Spell*, where Edward longs to be in the place of gratification; he is always looking in on love and desire from the outside and trying to work out its logic, mechanisms and procedures, but it constantly eludes him. He is given one glimpse and experience of what a life of gratified desire might be like, and then it is taken away from him. There's something terribly fatalistic about that but of course the position of being on the outside is an interesting one for the writer, for the characters he creates as observers and interpreters. It's a commonplace of fiction to turn on the revelation of something that's been hidden – and it's actually a mechanism that I have come to mistrust, and I deliberately don't use it now. *The Folding Star* is very deliberately permeated by a sense of secrecy and the unspoken. Characters observe each other from their own private worlds but find it very difficult to communicate.

INT: In *The Folding Star* there is very much a sense of Edward Manners being aware of being looked at and constant references to him looking in mirrors. Descriptions of the Hermitage are very self-consciously realised and almost operatic in scope. It's as if the men are all taking part in a huge dramatic performance. John Berger comments that women are constantly aware of themselves being looked at and that they always see themselves through the eyes of others. Are the gay men protagonists in this book in the same position as women in that respect?

AH: Yes, there is equally something narcissistic about a lot of them; the reassurance is part of it, but of course reassurance doesn't always work. I suppose Edward has a very poor self-image and there is a deliberate discrepancy in the book between his own low sense of his attractiveness and appeal and the fact that others do find him attractive. He is in a constant state of anxiety about his own desirability. And beyond that there are points about the intensity of looking, coming together and being able to get on with each other. The narcissistic dimension of gay life can be traced in all sorts of ways; it goes back to the fact that there is something fundamentally narcissistic about gay relations, not looking at someone who is your physical and sexual opposite. I suppose that does add an interesting dimension to the idea of looking in the mirror and at other people. At quite another level it's in the nature of sustaining relationships that the other person gives you back an element of self and it enhances your sense of self-worth. But obviously Edward and Will are both very solitary characters who live predominantly in the worlds of their own desires; they are not social characters, and so that element of self-inspection takes on more importance.

INT: You could say that many of your characters are labouring under some sort of illusion or spell in that respect. Hugh says, 'The thing about spells is that you don't know at the time if they're good ones or bad ones.' What is the spell they are all labouring under?

AH: It's different things for different people. I think I was trying to write about the idea that everybody has notions in their head, even quite preposterous notions, which lead them through life and guide them towards what they think they want to do, which they might or might not be able to achieve. People surrender themselves with varying degrees of illusion to fantasies of one kind or another. Edward is always surrendering responsibility for his life to the driving force of his obsession; in *The Spell* I perhaps show how different ideals of love give meaning to the characters' lives and acknowledge that sometimes people have great potential for happiness.

INT: *The Spell* marks a departure from your use of first-person narrative. Does the change in narrative style allow you to give more insight into some of the areas that you write about?

AH: I think it does because you can free yourself from the monological constraints of the first person. The first person is wonderful for other sorts of freedoms, such as exploring the consciousness and creating in great detail the emotional and imaginative world of a person, and colouring everything that happens in the book by its filtration through their mind and feelings. At the same time it does box the writer in and you long to be able to juxtapose those experiences with others to which you don't have any access, unless you use a device like Lord Nantwich's diaries. I very much wanted to get away from those constraints, and I found a liberating freedom in the change of narrative voice.

INT: Is it difficult to evade those labels that are most firmly attached to you as a writer, such as 'Alan Hollinghurst the gay writer'. Do you find that a problem?

AH: I don't think it is a problem, it's only annoying if it is taken to suggest that the gayness of the writer is the only interesting thing about the books. It's true that from the start, though I was writing about all sorts of things, it was explicitly from a gay viewpoint; that was a given, just as the heterosexuality of most authors is. When my first two books appeared that probably seemed a striking thing about them, but to me it was only a beginning, it didn't define the whole interest of the books. And so there is a sense in which 'gay writer' can be a reductive label, but I can't honestly say that I get hot under the collar about it.

INT: *The Swimming-Pool Library* does appear on the list of greatest gay novels. Dorothy Allison says that such novels 'contribute to the understanding of the outsider mentality'. What are your thoughts on this comment and are such lists ever valuable?

AH: Their only value would be to point people who want to read about particular things to books that they might not have heard of. Gay literature as a genre, I suspect, will prove to have been significant for only quite a short period of time, though, of course, gay writers will carry on writing about their experiences. We were talking earlier of it being novel and challenging to write about these topics, but there has been a huge sociological change in the past twenty years, and since my first book came out. I'm not saying we are now living in a perfect world of acceptance, but it seems that some of the fighting necessities of gay writing have gone and its future will probably be as a rich part of a different and constantly evolving literature. Its distinctness, as a genre in opposition, will become less and less as time goes by.

INT: Do you ever feel you have obligations to your readers in terms of how you portray certain issues? It is briefly mentioned that Robin's partner dies of an AIDS-related disease and Dawn in *The Folding Star* has AIDS but dies in a car accident.

AH: Those two things were gestures on my part, acknowledging the subject but showing that I wasn't going to make it a central part of my narrative. It wasn't actually the subject that I was dealing with in those books. I have avoided writing about AIDS because I couldn't convince myself that I had found a way to do it. I couldn't find a way to do so that seemed to me artistically satisfactory; but of course I hope that doesn't make my books weakly evasive. I admit I resist the idea that one must write about this, or any other, issue. If someone tells you that you must write about something of course the impulse is often to do the opposite.

INT: Your male protagonists are often high-minded and have an intellectual rigour – for example Robin and Alex in *The Spell*, Edward Manners and Paul Echevin in *The Folding Star*, Will Beckwith in *The Swimming-Pool Library*. Can you talk a little about the tension between high idealism and promiscuous sexual urges in your characters and the humour that's inherent in that tension?

AH: I think that tension has always been part of the pattern of my fiction and it's there in the subject matter and the style and the vocabulary. Sometimes I go back and read some parts of my novels, which I know some people have read completely straightfaced, and I find myself laughing. This is something which struck me particularly with the reviews of my last book because so much of *The Spell* does depend on tone of voice, which I can hear very clearly but perhaps a lot of readers can't and therefore don't appreciate its ironies.

INT: One critic described *The Spell* as Jane Austen on ecstasy and I suppose your writing could be seen as a variation on the middle-class novel of manners. A sort of 'reader I fucked him' rather than 'reader I married him'. Working-class characters are a bit thin on the ground in your novels (apart from Beckwith's fancies in *The Swimming-Pool Library* and Terry, the handyman in *The Spell*). Is it that working-class homosexuality is less acceptable than the homosexuality honed on the playing fields and in the public schools of the establishment males?

AH: *The Swimming-Pool Library* directly addresses the old idea that gay men are linked across barriers of class and race by sexuality and puts it up against a system in which the forces of class are still extremely powerful. It is very interesting finding what has been acceptable or possible at different times, in terms of cross-class relationships. It's very different from two men from the same sort of social background being able to forge a relationship. It's something that I have touched on consciously, but I suppose I tend to write about a world in which I have lived and moved, and also about one socially 'superior' to that. From the novelist's point of view, of course, people who have money and connections give scope for fictional freedoms which working-class characters don't. I think the truth is that I don't know a lot about working-class life and so, without its being at all a schematic decision, it hasn't arisen as a subject in my books.

INT: The idea of mapping yourself on a place figures strongly in your work. The terrain of the place through which the characters move seems an integral part of who and what they are. Is that quite deliberate?

AH: Yes, very much so. I am very interested in the atmosphere of places and buildings, and it is certainly an essential part of how I think and feel about my life; episodes in my life seem saturated with the atmosphere of a particular place. I always put in a lot of stuff in which I am interested and of course I hope to make it interesting to the reader. I have been interested in architecture since I was a child, and it is a richly available subject to me – I don't have to research it. I don't like research much, I do very little of it in general, and the huge palpable presence of research is something that I rather hate in contemporary fiction. Of course you have to know something about your chosen area or period, and I do read lightly around what I'm going to do, but then I almost try to forget what I have researched, so that the material regains a quality of the imagined, or of things recalled from one's own past. If you describe things with enough clarity and conviction, then people tend to believe them.

INT: Are there any other writers you admire or who have influenced you in any way, and who do you consider interesting amongst the current crop of writers?

AH: All through my teens I read poetry much more than fiction. I didn't read 'proper' fiction like Jane Austen until I was much older and went to university. I read Tolkien obsessively in my early teens, and then P. G. Wodehouse, but my adolescence was saturated above all in the Romantic poets and Victorian poets. I read Keats, Wordsworth and Tennyson in particular all the time when I was a schoolboy, and I still do read poetry at least as much as I read fiction. So I don't think I had fictional influences early in my life. I think it's easier for readers to see who your influences are than it is for you yourself. I have never modelled myself directly on anyone or sought to write like someone else, but at the same time I know that what I write is quite literary in its bearings and it does make reference to all sorts of other literary figures and traditions. I read very little contemporary fiction actually, and what I do is mainly work by friends like Graham Swift and Edmund White, Candia McWilliam or Edward St Aubyn. I read a great deal more in the literature of the past, and in the French and the Russians. Of American writers Henry James has long been one of my favourites, though he can be dangerous to read when one is writing oneself: his rhythms get into one's brain. I like going back and rereading. I suppose, thinking about it, I have read quite a lot but I'm not a voracious reader, I'm not someone who always has his head in a book. I still read a lot of poets, whose music is very much in my system. I revisit them constantly.

INT: There are quite a lot of references to poets such as Milton, Wordsworth, Keats and Blake in your novels.

AH: Yes, I quote and allude quite a lot. There are semi-secret references. *The Folding Star* is about someone soaked with poetry as an adolescent and whose whole experience of growing up is woven in with the moods and phrases of poems.

INT: Your personal history is bound up with reading as much as writing it seems. Do you have any thoughts on what is the key to a successful novel?

AH: For me how fiction is written has always been more important than story. I sometimes leave even a very good novel unfinished because all I really want from it is the atmosphere, the sense of its imaginative world. I also think wit is very important, not just humour, but a pervasive sense that the author is in control, that he knows the meaning of words and of what he does with them, and that his voice is alive with its own ironies. I like writers who, whilst not being stingy, don't waste words, and who use the right words in the right place. This is the essence of the short story, I suppose, and some of the writers I most admire now are short-story writers like Alice Munro, Tobias Wolff and Helen Simpson, all in their different ways wonderfully rich and utterly economical.

INT: You said that James is one of your favourite writers. What is it about his work do you think makes it so successful?

AH: What excites me above all, perhaps, is the extraordinary intelligence that he brought to every aspect of his writing. The task is performed with an insight and awareness the equal of that that he brings to his characters and their situations.

INT: Will you talk about your current projects?

AH: I've just finished a novel, *The Line of Beauty*, which is set in the mid-1980s, mainly in London; it starts just after the 1983 election, and finishes just after the 1987 election; in a sense it picks up from the moment when *The Swimming-Pool Library* ends, but its tone and perspectives are very different. It's about an intelligent but innocent and very susceptible young man whose love of beauty leads him astray in the amoral muddle of that decade. One of the main characters is a Tory MP, with whom his life becomes closely involved.

Select criticism

Alderson, David. 'Desire as Nostalgia: The Novels of Alan Hollinghurst', in David Alderson and Linda Anderson, eds, *Territories of Desire in Queer Culture: Refiguring Contemporary Boundaries*. Manchester: Manchester University Press, 2000.

Bradley, John R. 'Disciples of St. Narcissus: In Praise of Alan Hollinghurst', *The Critical Review* 36 (1996), pp. 3–18.

Brown, James N. 'Race, Class, and the Homoerotics of *The Swimming-Pool Library*', in Patricia M. Sant and John C. Hawley, eds, *Postcolonial and Queer Theories: Intersections and Essays*. Westport, CT: Greenwood, 2001.

Chambers, Ross. 'Messing Around: Gayness and Loiterature in Alan Hollinghurst's *The Swimming-Pool Library*', in Judith Still and Michael Worton, eds, *Textuality and Sexuality: Reading Theories and Practices*. Manchester: Manchester University Press, 1993.

Cooper, Brenda. 'Snapshots of Postcolonial Masculinities: Alan Hollinghurst's *The Swimming-Pool Library* and Ben Okri's *The Famished Road'*, *Journal of Commonwealth Literature* 34: 1 (1999), pp. 135–57.

Corber, Robert J. 'Sentimentalizing Gay History: Mark Merlis, Alan Hollinghurst, and Cold War Persecution of Homosexuals', *Arizona Quarterly: A Journal of American Literature, Culture, and Theory* 55: 4 (Winter 1999), pp. 115–41.

Sinfield, Alan. 'Culture, Consensus and Difference: Angus Wilson to Alan Hollinghurst', in Alistair Davies and Alan Sinfield, eds, *British Culture of the Postwar: An Introduction to Literature and Society, 1945–1999*. London: Routledge, 2000.

5 Hanif Kureishi

Nahem Yousaf and Sharon Monteith

Hanif Kureishi's writing career began in 1976 when he was only 22 and wrote a play called *Soaking the Heat*. By 1980 two of his plays had been accepted by the Royal Court theatre in London and a third produced on BBC radio. Recognition was swift, with Kureishi becoming writer-in-residence at the Royal Court and winning the George Devine Award in 1981. He was nominated for an Academy Award for his film screenplay *My Beautiful Laundrette* in 1985 and followed its success with *Sammy and Rosie Get Laid*, both directed by Stephen Frears. Kureishi settled in to write his first novel, *The Buddha of Suburbia*, which was published to critical and popular acclaim in 1990. In the years that have followed, Kureishi has published across a wide range of genres – short stories, music journalism and essays – and continued to write novels and screenplays. He directed a film based on his screenplay of *London Kills Me* in 1991, and the film of his novel *Intimacy* (directed by Patrice Chereau in 2001) won a Golden Bear Award at the Berlin Film Festival.

Kureishi has been a controversial figure primarily because his subject matter often deals with those communities that have been overlooked or under-represented in British creative arts. But it would be incorrect to assume that any controversy attached to him arises because his representations of Asians are unsympathetic or one-sided. Instead, it would be more accurate to say that he represents those members of society who are doubly or triply marginalised: the homosexual or drug-dealing Asian, the fanatical second-generation Muslim or the voiceless, divorced father. For bringing these characters to life in fiction and films, he has sometimes been attacked by a white majority and an Asian minority. The obvious defence mechanism against such attacks is to return to the position of the storyteller who does not choose to be a spokesman for a particular minority community or a particular generation. As he says below, Kureishi eschews labels and would prefer his work to be judged on its aesthetic merits rather than as an exemplificaton of a series of '-isms'. Readers familiar with Kureishi's creative output will know that a rich seam can be mined, in which spiky explorations of identity politics, Thatcher's Britain, minority–majority relations, the place of Islam in the UK, sexual relationships and the role of fathers in and outside of family units may all be discovered.

Key works:

My Beautiful Laundrette and Other Writings. London: Faber & Faber, [1986]
   1996.
'The Buddha of Suburbia'. *Harpers* 274: 16, 1987.
Sammy and Rosie Get Laid. London: Faber & Faber, 1988.
The Buddha of Suburbia. London: Faber & Faber, 1990.
Outskirts and Other Plays. London: Faber & Faber, 1992.
The Black Album. London: Faber & Faber, 1995.
The Faber Book of Pop (ed. with Jon Savage). London: Faber & Faber, 1995.
Love in a Blue Time. London: Faber & Faber, 1997.
Intimacy. London: Faber & Faber, 1998.
Sleep With Me. London: Faber & Faber, 1999.
Midnight All Day. London: Faber & Faber, 1999.
Gabriel's Gift. London: Faber & Faber, 2001.
The Body and Seven Stories. London: Faber & Faber, 2002.
Dreaming and Scheming: Reflections on Writing and Politics. London: Faber &
   Faber, 2002.
www.hanifkureishi.com (Kureishi's website, where some of his stories, essays
   and ideas first appear).

INT: Your interests are eclectic: you have cited African American and
Russian novelists, short-story writers such as Maupassant and
contemporaries – like Rushdie who influenced you. How do you find
your own voice as a writer?

HK: I do have my own voice but I can only tell you that I am naturally
influenced by everything I hear and read. I guess you might say that is
the postmodern condition. There is inevitably such a range of
influences and associations, as there is in Salman Rushdie's work too,
for example. I would say my father was the key influence but Rushdie
was important in that he knew the screenplays but felt that the novel
was the thing to work on in a sustained way and he told me I should
get writing one! I was a bit stung to begin with but I remember it
fondly. I was always just about to start on a novel and then I did, *The
Buddha of Suburbia*.

INT: Were you surprised by *Buddha*'s overwhelming success? And how do
you feel about its endurance as a classic of contemporary fiction?

HK: I am pleased it has held up. I wanted to write a book that people would want to read ten years later. But I am also pleased that works like *Buddha* and *My Beautiful Laundrette* helped to open the publishers' doors for other writers, because you forget that when I started writing people asked, 'Why are you writing about *Asians?* Who is interested in minorities? You'll never be successful writing about Asians.' You can't believe it now but when *My Beautiful Laundrette* came out it proved it was possible to make a film about Asian people that other people wanted to see: people went to see it and it was popular and made money. It is hard to get into that position in the first place. I remember applying for a bursary and being told, 'You are going to be in a writers' ghetto if you write about Asian people. Don't do that.' It was really insulting and offensive. So it is important to me, and I think to others who get through to publishers now. A novel like Zadie Smith's *White Teeth* can be a huge hit now, whereas what we write used to be described as 'Commonwealth Literature' – and to be located in that way is a form of ghettoisation.

INT: You have managed to deconstruct that ghettoisation in innovative ways. For example, Jay, the protagonist of *Intimacy*, doesn't wear his ethnicity on his sleeve so the reader is quite surprised to discover some way into the book that he is of mixed heritage.

HK: You expect to recognise ethnicity but no one says that a white character is white. It can unsettle the reader. There are always expectations. Asian people aren't 'Asian' for me any more than white people are 'white' for white people. They are just people. You couldn't get too caught up in issues of representation and continue to write.

INT: But the burden of representation did fall on you. There were those who expected you to smash stereotypes and create only positive representations.

HK: Yes, I was in New York when *My Beautiful Laundrette* came out and people demonstrated, marching up and down outside the cinema, shouting that the film was a slur and that there were no gay Asians (a gay Asian man falls in love with an ex-National Front member). But you can understand where they were coming from since there had been virtually no representation of Asians in the media. The answer is more diverse representation which the film helped to establish, I hope. In the end, you can't write to anybody else's ideas. If other people think Asians should be represented in a certain way, then they can write their own stories.

INT: So is there never a sense of a writerly obligation, or self-censorship?

HK: The self-censorship goes on all the time, to do with issues of style, taste, judgement, character. But I would never try to imagine what the world might want or not want. To try to fit in with it would prevent you from writing anything. For example, does the world want a film about a gay Nazi running a launderette? The work creates the market rather than the other way around, as with, for example, postcolonial writing where the works create the interest and the label comes later. When you imagine a mixed-race Asian living in the South London suburbs, you can't ask if anyone *wants* to read about him because no one *has* previously written about him, so you can't know.

INT: Your humour is earthy, salty, farcical at times. Can you say something about humour in *The Buddha of Suburbia* especially?

HK: I guess you develop your humour from your family directly out of the sense of humour your parents have. But I also grew up on British sitcoms. When you're sitting at home in Bromley you tend to mostly watch *Dad's Army* and *On the Buses* and *Please, Sir!* and all that stuff. That was the humour of my time in the 1960s and 1970s: in Bromley you didn't go and watch films directed by Godard, you watched *On the Buses*! My humour is very British in that sense. Any writer's humour comes from the sort of person you are – just as your whole style, the language you use and the characters you create come from your own character and how you see the world. The humour in my work has certainly changed over the years. *The Buddha of Suburbia* is a comic novel in a way that *Intimacy* quite clearly is not. Humour depends on your mood, on what the subject is, and on what you're thinking about at the time. I think the humour in *Buddha* comes from the point of view of a young man. When you're a kid adults are hilarious, your teachers all seem to have one leg and one eye and they're just funny. And you sort of deconstruct the world as a kid: you deconstruct the power and authority of the world by mocking it. People's parents are very funny to their kids. My children just look at me and they laugh. They think that the things I do are hilarious and I don't realise that I'm doing anything that might be conceived as funny. You can see the same things happening through the generations: you are just as idiotic to them as your parents were to you and so on. When you become the teacher yourself – when you become middle-aged and have only got one eye and one leg yourself – it is not so funny and the world becomes more complicated and more painful.

INT: Memory and history seem to play an important role for you.

HK: I think the history you remember is first and foremost your parents' lives: my father's life in India, my mother's during the Second World War. They were two quite different people coming together after the war in a bombed-out London, then having my sister and me and worrying about how we would fit in. Then there was the racism of the 1960s and Enoch Powell. Where your own life and that of your family intersects with general history is significant in terms of personal, psychological and social history.

INT: In *Intimacy* you write: 'The dream or nightmare of the happy family haunts us all. It is one of the few utopian ideas we have these days.' Are you writing in part against the fetishisation of the nuclear family?

HK: I was thinking the other day about the idea of the family that we grew up with in the 1950s and 1960s. The idea of the solid family that my generation had inherited was really breaking up by the 1980s when people like Margaret Thatcher and Ronald Reagan began to proselytise it. I remember being very puzzled by why Ronald Reagan and Margaret Thatcher in particular went on and on about the family. The whole idea of family by the 1980s was *clearly* breaking down and that is partly chronicled in *The Buddha of Suburbia* and later more seriously and in other ways in the other books like *Midnight All Day*, *Intimacy* and *Gabriel's Gift* where the problems of sustaining a relationship are described. Family was probably a fantasy in the first place. The whole idea rested on the woman being at home and the man going out to work while the kids were at school. There are very few people who live in that precise way in nuclear families.

INT: In the early work there are alternative 'families' – communes like Jamila's house in *Buddha*, Danny/Victoria's trailer park in *Sammy and Rosie* and the posse in *London Kills Me*. Do you see the nuclear family mediating into other forms – strangers or social outcasts coming together? Are you testing the boundaries of the 'family'?

HK: Growing up in the 1950s and 1960s and being involved on the left, and with hippies, I was very aware that my mates were thinking about new ways of living, particularly in that period after university and before, usually, you have kids yourself. I knew a lot of people living in housing associations, other people in communes and others involved in all kinds of sexual relationships, for instance, particularly the gay movement in the 1970s. I was very interested and involved in thinking about whether there were other ways in which to live without living in the traditional nuclear family. But I think people are still hypnotised by that idea. I don't think it's much of a reality and it's a dangerous idea in lots of ways because it makes people feel like failures. That is how 'family' has often been used, particularly by Thatcher: to make people in single families think that they were not as good as those in traditional families. I was extremely interested in the ways that the family was used politically in the 1980s.

INT: One cultural critic, Michael Neve in *The Age of Anxiety*, has argued that if we could stop fetishising the family unit, homesick fathers might have a better hearing. It seems to me that the non-custodial parent, still almost always the father, is a figure you have begun to rescue from obscurity in your recent work.

HK: I think that before feminism it was a bad deal: the men got the work and the women got the kids and there wasn't much sharing either way. So, the women missed out on the work and the men missed out on the kids. In a way under Thatcherism a lot of that changed, partly because of mass unemployment whereby men were at home and women did other kinds of work to make do. Inadvertently, people were able to experiment with different modes of living. I guess I'm interested in men because I'm a bloke myself but also because I was very interested in the revolutions of my time: for gays, women, blacks and Asians – with people becoming aware of their positions. And white blokes got rather left out of that. But, of course, when everybody else's position changed, the white bloke's position changed as well. So I try to write from his point of view as well and to examine the fallout.

INT: So, is a feature of your writing agenda a study of masculinity in crisis? Stephen in *Sleep With Me* and Roger in 'Umbrellas', for example.

HK: I think as a writer you look for the moment of crisis because it is so dramatic. When you think about how you're going to construct a text, you think of the moment when something is breaking down and you'll go in at that point. Say, in the film *My Son the Fanatic* where the main character is a taxi-driver: you look for the moment when his life is falling apart because for a writer that is dramatic. You look for the moment when he has to make lots of difficult decisions about who he wants to be. It's partly to do with craft, about where you start a story and about what you look for and where the story begins: where do you start? Where do you go in? It is about looking for the moment when somebody's life is falling apart and they have to think about who they are, what they believe and who they want to be and what sort of relationships they have. You can enter a marriage that is in crisis and think what do these people really want? Who do they want to be now? As a writer I try to go in at that point of crisis and then I can go back or forward and see what's happening.

INT: How do you feel about critical labels being attached to you in general? I'm thinking specifically of your work being labelled 'postcolonial'. Is it a term you can embrace?

HK: It's something you have to live with; it is going to happen. You write stuff and send it out and people are going to do things with it. That's fine and up to them but if you try to engage with them then that's when it gets difficult. For example, I can't think about myself as a postcolonial writer. When I go upstairs to my study, I think 'What do I want to write about today?' I can't think about myself or my work theoretically. I have to go to a concrete object: two people fighting over an umbrella. Then the writing comes alive. There are two aspects to writing: one is the creative aspect and the other is that it is a business in the sense that I have to support my family and that's the side of it where I send stuff out into the world and people make of it what they will. I think the postcolonial label has always bothered me slightly because, to me, it is a narrow term. And so much of my work is not about that and so you feel that you're being squashed into a category that you don't quite fit and you fear that there are lots of other aspects of your work which people might then be ignoring. But I'm not going to get hung up about that or bother about it too much. Perhaps people will get bored with postcolonialism and carry on reading my stuff. I don't think of V. S. Naipaul as a colonial or postcolonial writer, I think of him in the same way as I think of Graham Greene. They're both great writers.

INT: Are there descriptors that you feel more closely define you as a writer? Would you be happier being described as a chronicler of London?

HK: Well, I like London and I like what goes on here. I'm interested in the idea of opening the door and not knowing whom you are going to meet or what's going to happen. Also, being a suburban boy, I've never lost the romance of London: the idea of coming to London and it always being exciting and it always being dull in the suburbs, which to me as a teenager it certainly was. Writers have to be interested in the inside of people – their minds – and in the outside – the world – and the conjunction of those two things. The city has always turned me on. There's always something else I want to describe. For example, writing about the 1980s, the film world, Soho, or the advertising business that I haven't written about yet. I think what is great about the novel is that you can go anywhere with it and do anything. It seems to me to be a wonderful form, almost better than any other form for conveying human experience. You can go into people's minds, the intricacies of their minds, describe shops, streets, anything. If I read a book about Paris in the nineteenth century I like those bits, the descriptive sections. The novel is the most capacious, the most sensual form.

INT: So how do you feel when a novel is transferred to the screen? In the adaptation of *Buddha*, the first-person narration is lost. Do other aspects concern you?

HK: The language is lost and for writers it is the most important thing. All writers go to a lot of trouble to put their words in a certain order and to catch the right words where possible, and of course, you lose that. But you gain lots of other things too. You get to see actors' faces; you get to see good acting and good directing when you see the text as a movie. I've always worked in film so it's not as if I feel that film is necessarily a degradation of the work. I thought Roger Michell did a really good job with the TV version of *Buddha* and it worked very well. Now when I think of *Buddha* I see the actors, and the text is mediated through them. The actors have become superimposed on the text.

INT: You have compiled an ensemble, a cast of characters, and had some important collaborative relationships too, haven't you?

HK: I have been lucky to work with some tip-top people in the theatre and in film: Howard Davis, Max Stafford-Clarke, Stephen Frears, Patrice Chereau, Udayan Presaud, for example. You have to rework, compromise and change when working with directors and I need the argument and the criticism to test my work. I enjoy good and important fights over material and I've enjoyed working with a set of actors who are associated with my work, like Roshan Seth, Naveen Andrews, Rita Wolf, Meera Syal, Steve Mackintosh. My film *The Mother* features Steve Macintosh again. It's a dull life being a writer so working in film and the theatre with actors is cheering and inspiring.

INT: You have also compiled a cast of characters who reappear.

HK: Yes, in *Gabriel's Gift* especially. I think you become really fond of them, you get to like them. They're all parts of your own self in some way but you also wonder how they develop and age. I guess what I'm interested in is time and how people change over time. I'd like to know what Karim is doing now or what Charlie Hero is really like now, and Karim and Charlie enter the story, which is about a boy whose father knew them in the seventies. It is inspiring for me to imagine what might have happened to them so I write about characters I created years ago. I like the fact that the audience is interested too so you have a relationship with readers who recognise what you are doing. I usually write a group of things – stories and novels – around a subject, like *The Black Album* and 'My Son the Fanatic' which go together. The short story 'Night Light' works with 'Sleep With Me' and *Intimacy*, then there's *The Buddha of Suburbia* and *My Beautiful Laundrette*. I tend to write around the same subject for a bit until I feel that I've said what I want to say. You circle around, rather like a painter who might do a sketch, a sculpture and a painting of the same subject, a face or a body, and experiment with the subject for a while before moving on to something else.

INT: You have also said that you measured out your life in pop music and that consequently music forms part of your cultural vocabulary.

HK: I did at the beginning. I don't think I do so now. It was so liberating for us at that time. Music was linked to so many other things, not just fashion but politics – in Eastern Europe and in the United States – the straight world, the weird world. It meant so much. Then, when I was writing *The Black Album*, I was listening to a lot of Prince and Madonna. It was a time in the 1980s when ambiguous sexuality was moving into the mainstream and subcultures were becoming mainstream. It was very odd how the Thatcherite–Reaganite energy was absorbing the weirdo stuff, turning people on to it but at the same time rendering it innocuous. Music can take you anywhere. I had been interested in the Beatles but I hadn't heard Little Richard. So then I listened to him and to John Lee Hooker, and to other black music of the 1950s. You begin with one thing and take up others. You might say that all culture works by appropriation. There's me, an Asian kid sitting in Bromley in my bedroom listening to the Rolling Stones, who appropriated black music, and at the same time I am reading James Baldwin. I'm in a sense reappropriating what I read when it comes to figure in *The Buddha of Suburbia*, having been influenced by all this other stuff as well. Clearly, you have to say there are all kinds of distinctions to be made about appropriation and influence.

INT: Thinking about *Intimacy*, I wondered whether it is really more about desire than intimacy? And in 'Blue, Blue Pictures of You' you actually have a character who considers writing 'a book of desire'.

HK: It is about the dream of intimacy, rather like we were talking about the dream of the family – or a fantasy of a certain kind of family. It is the idea or ideal that you might have that haunts you that you pursue but never quite catch up with. So, therefore, the story is about failed intimacy or the desire for intimacy. It is certainly about desire but what it is a desire *for* I'm not entirely sure: certainly for recognition rather than union, being recognised, being seen, being understood. The film is an adult film. I always thought it should have a 35 certificate. It is quite a dark film, not a film for eighteen-year-olds eating popcorn. Films at the moment seem to be so formulaic. When you see a film like this, it feels dark, strange and very unusual.

INT: Interviewed in the *Guardian*, Alexander McClintock – the partner of Kerry Fox, the actress in *Intimacy* – described the film as an example of 'sublime ugliness'.

HK: I have written an essay about the film, 'The Two of Us' [also 'Filming *Intimacy*' in *Dreaming and Scheming*]. It is really about Patrice Chereau and me thinking about people like Francis Bacon and Lucian Freud, about flesh – real flesh as opposed to advertising flesh. The idealisation and use of sex in the media seems to be corrupt as opposed to what bodies and sexuality are really like in real people, which I try to write about more seriously. This film is more like that – more like a Freud painting and that's the ugliness. There are real human bodies and real people, real struggles over desire that you don't usually see in the cinema. It is a composite of 'Night Light', 'Strangers When We Meet' and *Love in a Blue Time*. I told Chereau to take what he wanted from the works and then we sat around and worked out a story. I did the story in that sense.

INT: Desire has been seen as the location of resistance to convention through transgressive sexualities and relationships, drug-fuelled passion, pornography. Is that how you conceive of desire – or is it simply a utopian project?

HK: I think that all western literature is probably about desire so it is a broad subject in that sense. *Anna Karenina* is all about desire and so is *Madame Bovary*. It is a question of people wanting things very badly, which often comes down to people wanting other people very badly. The literature then becomes an exploration of the way that your desire for other people is always constrained by society, in that you are not allowed to desire certain people, certain things.

INT: You could say that *Anna Karenina* and *Tess of the D'Urbervilles* are constrained by romance plots, though, while you are not limited in that precise way.

HK: That's an interesting thing to say. The form of the novel has changed and I'm also working across a number of genres. What is common is the idea that desire is transgressive, as you say: Madame Bovary does not love her husband but she does love people who are not her husband. In *My Son the Fanatic* the main character is no longer in love with his wife but he loves a prostitute, which is transgressive in itself. But what should we make of it? It becomes not only an emotional, sexual problem but a social problem too, and that is when a novelist gets interested and worried and starts to think about how desire works in society, not only in the minds and bodies of the people involved.

That's a question that we are all interested in: what do we do with desire? What shapes does it follow and how does it run? How transgressive does it have to be to continue to be exciting? For Sigmund Freud all desire is transgressive and incestuous.

INT: In your early work desire is set against impending social crisis, as in *Sammy and Rosie* and *My Beautiful Laundrette*. But with the later work there is a stronger emphasis on the interior worlds of the characters.

HK: I suppose different kinds of desire are transgressive and dangerous in different ways. Let's say being gay in London today is not like being gay in Afghanistan so it depends where you locate the characters. During the 1980s, Thatcher, it seemed to a lot of us, was trying to introduce, in shorthand, 'old-fashioned morals'. Therefore desire seemed very important to write about then. So you combine two gay blokes running a launderette, which is the entrepreneurship she wanted, and you make it transgressive. The social stuff *has* fallen away to a certain extent.

Also my work has got more pared down. I think that often happens to artists: you become very interested in economy, doing things as economically as you can, and the wrong word or too many words offends you. I think you look for new styles. I am much more interested in a piece of writing that is broken up, fragmented, unfinished. Sometimes I look at my notes and think why would I even bother to organise these notes into a fluid page? I like the spaces between the notes. I leave three spaces between this chunk of prose and the next. I like it looking like that on the page. You show it to people and they tell you that you can't publish it as it is not 'written' yet, but it is the fact that it is *not* written that interests me.

But then to follow through, you may be moving away from the public. I guess my writing has always been quite conventional. I start at the beginning and move all the way through – just like the novels I read as I grew up. But now I am much more interested in the experimental, not for its own sake but because I like the look of the words on the page in that way – the gaps, the unfinished bits. The writing is like some of the later work of Miles Davis: it sounds cacophonous to other people. It may sound like banging on pots but it is interesting to him. It is quite difficult, particularly when you are an established writer, to decide how far you can go in terms of your relationship with the audience. I liked *Intimacy* being a rough book in that sense: the cruelty, the fragmentation, the lack of smoothing out or over. People have said the book is so cruel and horrible, the people in it are so nasty and I say, 'Well, that's what it's like.' I wanted the book to be an experience. If I wrote a book now about a relationship that split up ten years ago, it would probably be overworked and too thought-out. I wanted to capture the roughness. The style you use has to reflect what is going on in the mind at the time of writing.

INT: You have begun to exploit new technology as well with your website.

HK: I guess so. Websites are good for certain things. You can publish stories and bits and pieces on them. Websites are great in that you can write something and bang it up straight away but people don't really know it is there unless you go to a lot of trouble to advertise. Books are still best. But you get a lag with books. I've got two books that my publisher hasn't yet got around to publishing that will turn up after a bit. You have to plan an advertising campaign and go to bookshops. 'Goodbye Mother', a story that was originally published in *Granta* and is now collected in *The Body*, I put on my site first. But I don't think I would put a novel on there.

INT: Would you mind talking about forthcoming or as yet unpublished work?

HK: I would like to write another book about race, starting from the 1970s and coming up to the present day. I thought it might be a saga but my books are getting shorter and more condensed. My work, as I say, is becoming really concentrated and I don't write the bits I don't choose to. How much should you explain? Will the audience move through the ideas with you? These kinds of questions don't go away as you continue into your writing career.

INT: Do you feel you are picking up new readers with short stories?

HK: Maybe. It is hard for me to get a sense of the readership. Sometimes I will go to a reading but I don't get much idea of the specific audience. Reviews don't tell you much about your readership either. It is not like sitting in a cinema where you can see and feel people responding to the film you have made. But I did a reading in Leeds recently and there were a few men who were talking about being separated from their wives and children and of the relationships they try – and sometimes fail – to build with them both. It did give me a sense that people might look for that stuff in my work.

INT: At one juncture in the screenplay for *Sammy and Rosie Get Laid* you say that you are 'no good at plots, at working out precisely what the story is'. How significant is plot in your writing?

HK: I am interested in movement and change, in development in a person or character. Plot is a much more mechanical unfolding according to some preconceived plan which I can never quite do. I'm writing and then I think, wouldn't it be great if so-and-so happened now, and I go off in another direction, often this seems disjointed or weird. With *Sammy and Rosie* the film moves all over the place and I rather like that. In a sense there are two sides to me: wanting the work to be crafted and liking to do weird things in the work. In *Gabriel's Gift* a painting comes to life and Gabriel speaks with his dead brother, for example. Really in that novel the weird aspects have to do with somebody going mad because their parents have split up and they are trying to hold the family together. Gabriel wants to be an artist but is unable to move outside of his own head. Later in the book, Gabriel stops feeling crazy because he begins to relate to other people and to the world outside. It is important to be part of wider relations. It is rather like being a writer: if you sit up in your office imagining for long enough, your relationship with the rest of the world could become tenuous. So you keep sane by having relationships.

INT: So Gabriel is rescued by the relationship he has with his father, which socialises him?

HK: Yes, and he is rescued by his general ability to make friends with other people. I think the writing always has to exist in relationship to others or it becomes obsessive, circular. It is not just self-expression. Literary form is important too, as recognised by others.

INT: You conceived of *Gabriel's Gift* as a children's book, didn't you?

HK: Yes, in that David Bowie wanted a book that he could then illustrate, but as I was writing it became more of an adult book. I have written one children's story, 'Ladybirds for Tea'. I think when you have children, you want to write for them and it wouldn't occur to you otherwise.

INT: Do you feel *Gabriel's Gift* re-established you after the controversy of *Intimacy*?

HK: *Intimacy* really bothers people where *Gabriel's Gift* does not. I think some reviewers were caught up in the *furor* around *Intimacy* (my own relationship and the reviews that focused on that instead of the work) and so haven't yet looked fairly and squarely at the book. Nor have they yet taken into consideration the fact that I was aware I was playing a literary game. I consciously wrote *Intimacy* in the form of a confession and was also aware that it might be read as 'Hanif Kureishi telling the truth about a relationship break-up'. That too is a literary construct, it is artificial. All one's work is autobiographical to the extent that it reflects one's interests. But the book hasn't yet been read as a move in a literary game, which is quite disappointing. It operates as a construct – written in the first person, constructed as a confession – and this is the basis on which it should begin to be evaluated. I wanted a book people could play with in that way. It is a text, not me. I am not the text.

INT: Does the cult of celebrity annoy you then? If you weren't famous, critics wouldn't have read the novel as autobiography, and you do have that ironic scene in the short story 'That Was Then' when Natasha challenges Nick for using her life in his book.

HK: I suppose it works both ways. Being a celebrity allows you to write books that people will read – which is what we all want. When I made money writing the screenplays for *My Beautiful Laundrette* and *Sammy and Rosie* I made enough money to allow me to take the time to write *The Buddha of Suburbia*, my first novel. But, on the other hand, celebrity can devalue what you do, as all celebrity does in a sense. It makes what you do appear one-dimensional.

INT: The last section of *Gabriel's Gift* is a kind of coda – a happy ending. In reclaiming what is comfortable at the heart of many families, it is perhaps the happiest ending you have written, isn't it?

HK: There aren't any happy endings in life but there are happy moments. Other pieces I have written are cheerful too, like the story 'Four Blue Chairs'. What you want as a writer is to write in different tones for your own pleasure. It isn't as if any one thing you write is your final testament. *Intimacy* isn't how I am feeling today, or even how I felt the day after it was finished. It isn't my last word on marriage, relationships, children. You write in light and dark.

Select criticism

■ Books

Kaleta, Kenneth. *Hanif Kureishi: Postcolonial Storyteller*. Austin: University of Texas Press, 1998.

Moore-Gilbert, Bart. *Hanif Kureishi*. Manchester: Manchester University Press, 2001.

Ranasinha, Ruvani. *Hanif Kureishi*. Plymouth: Northcote House, 2002.

Yousaf, Nahem. *Hanif Kureishi's The Buddha of Suburbia*. New York and London: Continuum, 2002. A longer version of the interview above appears in this book.

■ Articles

Ball, John. 'The Semi-Detached Metropolis: Hanif Kureishi's London', *Ariel: A Review of International English Literature* 27: 4 (Oct. 1996), pp. 7–27.

McCabe, Colin. 'Interview: Hanif Kureishi on London', *Critical Quarterly* 41: 3 (1999), pp. 37–56.

Gardner, Geoff. 'Nature of Keeping Awake: Hanif Kureishi and Collaborative Filmmaking', at www.sensesofcinema.com

Sandhu, Sukdev. 'Pop Goes the Centre: Hanif Kureishi's London', in Laura Chrisman and Benita Parry, eds, *Postcolonial Theory and Criticism*. Cambridge: Brewer, 1999, pp. 133–54.

Spivak, Gayatri. 'Sammy and Rosie Get Laid' in *Outside the Teaching Machine*. London: Routledge, 1993, pp. 243–54.

Yousaf, Nahem. 'Hanif Kureishi and "The Brown Man's Burden"', *Critical Survey* 8: 1 (1996), pp. 14–26.

6

Bernard Mac Laverty

Sharon Monteith and Jenny Newman

Bernard Mac Laverty is the acclaimed author of four novels and four collections of short stories. He was born in Belfast and worked for ten years as a medical laboratory technician before going to Queens University, where he studied English Literature. In 1975 he moved to Scotland, living first in Edinburgh and then on the Isle of Islay – the setting for *Grace Notes* – before moving to Glasgow. In Scotland, he worked as a teacher before becoming a full-time writer. Two of his novels, *Lamb* and *Cal*, have been successfully adapted into films, with Mac Laverty writing the screenplays and Pat O'Connor and Colin Gregg directing. Mac Laverty has enjoyed considerable success with a series of BBC television plays as well as radio plays (often adapting his own short stories) and a drama documentary (*Hostages*, filmed for Granada in 1992). His interest in classical music led to his own radio programme, called *Grace Notes* after the novel that inspired it. Most recently, Mac Laverty has begun to direct: his first project is a short film, *Bye-Child*, deriving from a poem of the same name by Seamus Heaney. Mac Laverty's awards and prizes include the Saltire Scottish Book of the Year Award for *Grace Notes*, which was also shortlisted for the Booker Prize, and the Scottish Arts Council Book Award for *Secrets and Other Stories*, *Lamb* and *A Time to Dance*.

Mac Laverty sets novels and stories in Northern Ireland and in Scotland, reflecting the journey he made from Belfast to Glasgow and the importance he attaches to roots and region. Pertinent, and often metaphysical, themes explored across his work include an autobiographical emphasis on Catholic boyhood in Belfast; the lonely misfit; the family in all its forms and father–son relationships in particular; the problematising of guilt and innocence and the often tragic tensions between Republicans and Loyalists that have characterised the Troubles in Northern Ireland. The importance of music and sound in Mac Laverty's work, which culminates in the award-winning *Grace Notes*, has been much acclaimed as an example of musical forms taking literary shape, as has Mac Laverty's facility in the same novel for capturing the interior life of a depressed young mother. *The Anatomy School* has been praised for combining a very different blend of dialogue and salty humour in the form of a much more traditional *Bildungsroman*. From novels to short stories, screenplays to radio, Mac Laverty has remained a consistently popular and admired proponent of both Irish *and* British fiction.

Key works

Secrets and Other Stories. Belfast: Blackstaff Press, 1977.
A Man in Search of a Pet. Belfast: Blackstaff Press, 1978 (for children).
Lamb. London: Cape. Belfast: Blackstaff Press, 1980.
A Time to Dance and Other Stories. London: Cape. Belfast: Blackstaff Press, 1982.
Cal. London: Cape. Belfast: Blackstaff Press, 1983.
The Great Profundo and Other Stories. London: Cape. Belfast: Blackstaff Press, 1987.
Walking the Dog and Other Stories. London: Cape. Belfast: Blackstaff Press, 1994.
Grace Notes. London: Cape. Belfast: Blackstaff Press, 1997.
The Anatomy School. London: Cape. Belfast: Blackstaff Press, 2001.
All Mac Laverty's work has been published in new editions by Vintage.

INT: In 1975 you moved from Northern Ireland to Scotland, thus giving yourself a kind of dual location. Do you see yourself as part of a Celtic diaspora?

BM: Somebody once asked me if I considered myself a Scottish writer or an Irish writer, and with the slightest of smiles I said, 'I bestride the Irish Sea like a colossus!' And the interviewer wrote it down without an exclamation mark! The major experiences of my life have had a Celtic connection; but if you say, 'I am an Irish writer', it has certain implications, elements of comedy, like, 'Oh, he must write about horses, and drunken scenes.' So I'm wary of how I view myself. When I left Belfast, I did want to go where there were other Celts.

When you talk to writers like Alasdair Gray, you understand very quickly that Scotland has a distinct oral culture, and the importance of the word and the way the Scots talk is very much the same as in Ireland. This place is only a short boat ride from Donegal, Antrim and Belfast, and over generations the migrants have come. Patrick MacGill in *Children of the Dead End* expresses that journey beautifully in 1914, and describes labouring in the countryside. So people have made the journey I made before. There's a very Irish feel to the west of Scotland, and to some extent it has some of the problems of sectarianism.

INT: In terms of sectarianism, you not only reconcile two locations, but also warring factions in the way you bring Protestants and Catholics together in your work – as in *Cal*, where an Irish Catholic man falls in love with a Catholic woman who is married to a Protestant police reservist, or in *Grace Notes* when Catherine, a Catholic, composes music which features the Lambeg drums played by Orangemen.

BM: If you grow up in a place like the North of Ireland trying to write and suddenly the whole place collapses, it is going to affect you to the core of your being. I was twenty-seven in 1969, and around me there was anarchy, murder and mayhem. You want to deal with that in writing but the events are so close to you that you can't. I waited ten years before I could write about the violence. I wrote about it in an oblique way in my first novel, *Lamb*, where Michael attempts to destroy the thing he loves in the same way that misdirected Republicanism was destroying the country. 'This is our country. This is what we love.' Yet they were blowing it to bits. It is about much more than religion. The Catholics were an under-population, and second-class citizens.

INT: Do you feel that being brought up a Catholic is useful for a writer?

BM: One of the things I feel about religion – in hindsight – is that it was a great thing to be involved in; it was a great upbringing. Growing up Catholic, I took symbols and words to be immensely important. For me it was like a James Joyce experience: I was sitting in the church reading my mother's missal when I came across the word 'concupiscence'. It nearly took up a whole line! I said to my mother, 'What's that?' and she said, 'Aw, stop – pay attention!'

But you fall into accepting the dominant ideas attached to symbols: that white means hope and red means blood, and that the water that baptises you is also a cleanser of your skin, and that at Easter, which is the best time, the church is completely blacked out, then the flame is passed from candle to candle spreading the light of Christ throughout the world. You fall into accepting lovely things like that, except they're not true. That's what hindsight brings. So you grow up with this imagery, and the layers it has, and the consciousness of the world, and then later on you come to doubt it, like Catherine does in *Grace Notes*. She has been in love with each facet of religion: the stained-glass windows, the architecture, the Gregorian chants. All the trappings of religion are still valuable to her, but their core has disappeared. In the same way she keeps shells, for their architecture: they may have had their living centres drawn out, but they are still worth looking at. Art is a way of looking at ourselves. We paint and record ourselves, and Catherine makes sounds with music. All the ways in which we attempt to explore what we are as human beings can become some kind of substitute for religion. Religion says, 'This is the answer, you do this, you live your life according to this, and it will result in an afterlife of eternal happiness.' But when that doesn't exist for us any more, we examine life, seeing the cruelties and the awfulness, and the injustices. Art is a reflection of that, and that's really what's left to us.

INT: So Catholic introspection was useful to you?

BM: I can imagine that introspection and the silence and self-examination that form part of that would be important to anybody. It's a kind of meditation really, that throws you back on yourself. But in my growing up I think my set of friends was much more important to me. There were five or six of us, and everybody had some kind of hobby or interest that they would push on the others. One friend was interested in opera, and he'd drag you into his front room and play you Mozart, and another guy was interested in philosophy and he would be reading Plato and Existentialism and exploring Sartre, and another friend was into theology and the priesthood, and I liked jazz, and I would listen to that and want to share the experience. So, as a group of people we were introspective, but we were learning from each other in a way the education system didn't allow for at all – although I remember we did have a good English teacher in our A-level year, who recommended us to go away and read Graham Greene and D. H. Lawrence (controversial enough writers in a 1950s Catholic school).

I remember the summer after leaving school I went to a seaside hotel to be a waiter. I took a library book of the poems of Gerard Manley Hopkins with me. Despite working from six in the morning till two the following morning I read it, not so much for the poems as the Notebooks at the back of that old Penguin volume. I so enjoyed the details, like drips of water, rain hanging from the undersides of railings and bluebells 'jostling' in the hands, precision words describing lovely things like that. I would tell my friends. We were a group of people passionate about learning who shared their experiences.

INT: Yet in your novels and short stories you often write less about groups and more of outsiders, like Brother Sebastian in *Lamb*, or Danny and Miss Schwartz in 'My Dear Palestrina', both of whom are misfits.

BM: Conformists are not the most interesting people. In 'My Dear Palestrina' Danny's father is very ordinary and reads the *Daily Express*, and it's hard to write about him in a sustained fashion. There seems to be more depth to a character like Danny's teacher, Miss Schwartz, not knowing where she's going – a conflicted person who has finally found a pupil who's really good and she doesn't want to lose this chance. It's hard to write about dull people. For instance, when Blaise walks into *The Anatomy School*, he's a striking figure invading an institution, like McMurphy in *One Flew over the Cuckoo's Nest* – I would hope. A stranger coming in is a way of communicating what the situation is in the story and commenting on it. Blaise is an outsider from everything who has been expelled from other schools, and so I find him very interesting.

INT: Despite his obvious intelligence you push him out of the novel quite quickly, and don't bring him back until the end. Why did you choose not to end the novel in the world of school, with some sort of resolution of the crisis over the examination papers?

BM: *The Anatomy School* had structural problems which I hope I solved. In *Grace Notes* the two parts had reflected each other – a sort of musical technique – and I didn't want to do that again. Instead, in *The Anatomy School* there are blocks of time, like the term, the weekend, the afternoon and one final night after Martin has left school when everything happens, the interminable first night he stays over at the laboratory where he works, does a night shift, and loses his virginity – and then all his friends turn up, including Blaise.

I'd intended to write a novel about twelve-to fourteen-year-old boys, and then some people said, 'You're writing a novel about your dad again.' And I wondered why. But then I realised: I was twelve when my father died; he died before I got to talk to him as an adult. As a child I'd just chattered to him, and had had no idea he was ill. Then he died of cancer, and my world became a completely different place. I wrote a story about it called 'Compensations', where two brothers are left with their grandparents while their mother and father go off to Lourdes, for the last Catholic throw of the dice. It was such a crucial time for me because I keep going back to it. Graham Greene says somewhere that everything important to a writer has happened to him before he is eighteen. I think he is right.

When I started to write I thought, 'I can try on different fathers. What was that one like? And him?' In one story you have a sensitive, gentle, religious man, and you think, 'Let's make the opposite! a real monster.' And you make a pig of a man who stabs his son's hand with a fork to correct his table manners.

If you take teenage boys as your subject, it is valuable to see them from both sides: as a pupil, scared witless, and as a teacher, equally scared witless. I only taught for five years, but I enjoyed that period. The first year was awful. I didn't know what I was doing, in a new school, and in a new country. They hadn't even given me a room, and I stored all my books in a locker in the toilet. I didn't really have a classroom, either, so the experience was physically and intellectually exhausting – running up and down corridors with thirty hardback copies of the book the class was working on. In the second year I gained enough confidence to do reasonably well, and five years later I was almost taking shortcuts. In 1981 I said to the education authorities, 'Could you give me a year off to write a novel?' They wouldn't, so I left. Organisations see creativity as a way of being cheeky.

INT: You deal not only with boys but with extremely innocent adults in your fiction, such as Michael Lamb, who is about to become terribly guilty.

BM: I said that the good aspect of Catholicism was that you grew up with language and image and symbol; but guilt is a real Catholic anchor – and it slows you down in a way! Confession was terrible. What happens to wee boys wanking, all that kind of stuff. The life of young Catholics in 1950s and 1960s Ireland was difficult: it involved going into dark boxes and telling grown men what you did with yourself, and then going off with girls and trying things out – just natural relationships – only to be told that you'd go to Hell as a result. It was nonsense. But we were naive enough, and un-Blaise-like enough, to believe it all and it influenced us. So in the last paragraph of *Cal* it is his Catholicism that dogs him, and he's grateful that he's going to be finally punished for what he has done. Huang Xaio Gang in *Grace Notes* calls Catherine 'Lady Macbeth' and I remember having a series of dreams where I killed somebody, or knocked somebody down in a car, and I still remember the guilty intensity of that imagined experience.

I wrote *Secrets* when I was in Edinburgh, and then I thought, 'God, I have to write a novel! What will I write a novel about?' Then one morning in the paper I read a murder trial of an Irishman. The judge said it was one of the saddest cases he'd ever had to preside over, because it aspired to be a father and son relationship. And I thought, how does somebody come to that extreme point? And my answer to that question was *Lamb*.

INT: Is yours a world where suffering can be redemptive, or are all your characters trapped?

BM: Cal just goes along with things, and I certainly experienced that kind of helplessness in Belfast. I see my other characters as trapped too, except for Catherine McKenna. She's trapped biologically and medically, in a way, but manages somehow to see some light through the dark. The fact that there are two parts to the book's structure means you can end on a high note before you realise that the *actual* end has been in the middle of the book when she relapsed into another depression. But it wasn't as bad as what she first suffered, so some small progress has been made – in the human condition, the way out of the blackness. . . . My whole idea of redemption has changed over time. You are fighting your own wee battles and looking for contentment and trying not to be depressed, you know, looking for joy. What was it that Raymond Carver said? Something like – to love and be loved, that is as much as we can hope for.

INT: The world of *Lamb* and *Cal* and that of many of your short stories is predominantly masculine. Why in *Grace Notes* did you suddenly shift to a feminine viewpoint?

BM: *Cal* has a father–son relationship and *Lamb* has a father and son, though not in the flesh, not biologically. When I came to write *Grace Notes* I thought, 'Maybe I should do a mother and daughter. Am I capable of doing that?' My background information came from the women who had surrounded me in my childhood: I was brought up in a house where I had a mother and a grandmother and a great aunt. Across the street was my Aunt Cissie, and Cousin Anne. I was surrounded by strong, talking women!

The novel was sparked off by a friend who is also a writer. She had to balance her writing with having babies. I think that was a starting point, and in a throwaway remark she made was the whole of the novel. She said, 'It's all right for you – you don't have to have the babies.' Biological production can get in the way of creativity and I was all right because I didn't have to have the children. I have also had an interest in music since the 1960s and that interest provided a momentum for the book. At the start of a novel you never know where it will go, you just push along – and I didn't know where I was going with *Grace Notes*. Apart from that throwaway remark about how much more difficult things could be for women, I think it began with a story about a woman who was in prison, falsely accused of Republican crimes (at one time there were seventeen such people). I wanted to write about a woman in that position. And then as the book grew I subtracted the bars of the prison, and it became a prison of the mind. I rejected the Republican thing altogether. See, you just push forward. I remember going down wrong paths, like Robert Frost's 'The Road Not Taken', and trying to get Catherine involved in relationships and thinking, 'No! that's terrible. Get back!' Then you scrap a week's work, go back, and try to get a feeling for moving forward in a new and different direction.

INT: The depth of her intelligence intrigued me more than the fact that she gives birth. She's more sophisticated than many of your male characters.

BM: I hope talking about this doesn't make me sound weird, but the admiration and love we have for the opposite sex is a way of expressing gratitude. *Grace Notes* was a creative exploration. It was broadcast on a BBC Radio 2 programme about music and novels as a huge two-hour play with Amanda Burton. They invited the composer who'd written the music to come to the studio and then asked her, 'Is this what it's like to be a young female musician?' And she said yes!

That was the book for which I did most research, in terms of music, reading about music, what a composer is saying, how music comes, and then a trawl of reading about obsessive compulsive disorder and postnatal depression. I came across this thing about Satie that he had scrawled in the margins of his manuscript: 'This piano piece should be played 840 times.' You find something like that, and it's valuable, because it fits the plot and it fits the character: the repetition of music is made to feel like compulsive thoughts. Then I attended an advertised composer's workshop at the BBC, with the Chinese composer Tan Dun. He worked on a stage with about ten music students. There were no musical instruments and he used breath and voice to compose – along with mouth pops and hand claps. He talked about pre-hearing and inner hearing. I was sitting rapt on the edge of my seat in a lecture on composition listening to people breathing. Tan Dun became the basis for the composer Huang Xiao Gang in *Grace Notes*. It was magic. Then one Saturday afternoon we wandered up to Glasgow University and saw a science fair for children. A man set up an experiment with lit candles on a small staircase. He told the kids a gas can be heavier than air, and that carbon dioxide will not sustain combustion. Then he poured a container of carbon dioxide down the staircase and the candles winked out one by one. I could hardly run home quickly enough to write it as an image of depression!

INT: Danny in 'My Dear Palestrina' and Catherine in *Grace Notes* are always listening for – and finding – sense through what they hear. Do you agree that this is a very particular facet of what you write about?

BM: Those two stories are both about music and people involved in music. Their hearing is therefore more acute than that of the rest of us. In *Grace Notes* I wanted the sense of creativity but I wanted the artists to be ordinary, so I didn't really mention music until page thirty or so. The novel begins with Catherine going down the steps from the house, and somebody whistling in the bus station, and then she gets the bus to the airport where somebody's sawing with a hand saw and a baby is crying. All those sounds assault the reader. And the first mention connecting Catherine with music is made by Geraldine, a family friend who is helping to clean the house. She waggles the fingers of her yellow rubber gloves and simply asks, 'How's the piano playing going?' The first time Catherine plays piano she is wearing an old blue housecoat and she sits at the instrument wrapped in a duvet. Hopefully the reader wonders whether music may be just a hobby of hers. And later you realise it's the centre of her whole life. And so I set up the premise of the novel through the acuteness of her hearing before introducing her musical talent. And I suppose the same kind of thing is happening in 'My Dear Palestrina', where the little boy is able to hear more acutely than anybody else around him.

INT: What about silence as an ambience out of which speech or music comes? Do you have a sense of the spaces between the notes and the silence between the words?

BM: If I've ever had an original thought, it might be that literature is the science of feeling. This occurs in an early story of mine called 'Hugo', where the Hugo of the title expresses himself thus: 'The artist analyses what feelings are, then in some way or other he tries to reproduce in the reader those same feelings. How much more subtle an experiment than overflowing an oul bath. How many feelings are there to reproduce, do you think? Is there a periodic classification of feelings? Nuances – that's the secret. The lines in the spectrum between pity and sympathy. Literature is the space between words. It fills the gaps that language leaves. English only has one word for love and yet how many different types of love are there in literature?'

And I do see writing as being about emotion. And that applies right across the board to, say, Kafka as well as Joyce. I can't continue with a book that doesn't move me in some way. If you listen to Bach you might say there's no sentiment whatsoever; but it's the structure which moves you. I suppose literature does that to you, too: creates pictures inside your head. You realise you can synchronise with those pictures and you come to an understanding, 'Yes, I know what's going on here.'

INT: You use the senses so much, in a visceral way. Even with the pornographic photographs in *The Anatomy School:* it's not just what's in them, but the texture of the paper when Martin touches them and later burns them. Is that something you're consciously working through: making the reader listen to the visual, or making us see what we hear?

BM: Photography is an element in my earlier stories. In *Cal* when the boy blinks it's as if he is taking a photograph of what he sees. The shutter clicks and he can later recall it as a vivid memory. Examining the world is art. Whatever form you use (be it photography or movies or painting) becomes your way of examining the human condition. My father had a darkroom set up in the house, and I had a summer job in a photo works cutting up negatives – and in haste, frequently across the middle! When you have that sort of knowledge in your armoury, you've got to use it.

INT: But you seem to find lots of different ways for your characters to register emotion too.

BM: I think the most relevant point was made by Willa Cather, who talked about what is expressed on the page without being named there. In other words, if you're writing about fear, you don't use the word itself, or the phrase, but you may describe sweaty hands or sharpness of breath. So the physical world is registered and that's how I register the five senses on the page. Another influence in the beginning was reading Michael McLaverty: it was the visual way that he wrote, the way of writing a physical world. I admired the pictures he created. They're more than pictures: they're composed of sound and smell and the other senses. It's the way that I write, and it's not an intellectual way. It's how we come into contact with the world, through the senses.

INT: In most of your stories and novels, including *The Anatomy School*, you create a lot of suspense. For example, when Martin steals the keys from Condor's room, the tension is almost unbearable. Do you aim to give your reader a gripping story?

BM: I think telling stories is so important – it's the way I was reared. One of the greatest feelings in the world is to open a book and feel that you're in the hands of someone who knows what they're doing. Like Brian Moore, for example. Four pages into a Brian Moore novel I think, 'Wow, we're away here.' The cliché is 'a page-turner', isn't it – a novel where you always want to know what happens next? That is crucial to what writing fiction is about, and I try to create that suspense. It works from sentence to sentence or even within the sentence – like a bomb. When Brian Moore starts the process off, you don't know where you're going to end up, and by the end of a sentence you may think, 'How did I get here? How did he bring me to this place or feeling?' That same thing happens in paragraphs and chapters and in the novel as a whole. All pleasures. The body has certain appetites so pleasure is always involved. The byproduct of the pleasure of eating is that it keeps us alive. Each bodily function has a pleasure attached to it and in a way that includes reading. And I think the function of literature, that page-turner of a novel, the narration of that story, is a pleasure that keeps us going. I cease reading a book that doesn't keep me engaged at some visceral level. So when I come to write, that's what I try to do. All art is a construct, in that you make the thing.

INT: Some of your titles function in a concrete way, like 'The Fountain-Pen Shop Woman' or 'Walking the Dog', which is about walking the dog, but so much more. But there are other titles – like 'A Time to Dance' – where the reader doesn't discover the significance of the title until the end of the story. Do your titles come first, and how significant are they?

BM: I find them difficult, and they nearly always come at the end of the writing process. It's like naming a child. When wee Julian is born, and doesn't have a name, you think, 'That's the baby', but when Julian's fourteen, Julian's Julian. You get used to the handle of a title. I read that Hemingway wrote down hundreds of titles when he'd finished a novel, then struck out the ones he didn't like until he only had one left. You try to pack as much into the story's label as possible. I've just finished a story in the voice of an old woman, and it's called 'The Assessment'. It is about an old woman who is being watched and assessed to see if she can look after herself or needs to be taken into care. Failure means that she will have to move into an old people's home. She thinks about her own life and tries to assess it. Assessment becomes the process of the story, the process of what's going on in the story, so you may have a title working in several ways at once. And then there are other titles that simply have a nice ring to them ('St Paul Could Hit the Nail on the Head'), a certain quality because there are certain words that are memorable in themselves ('The Miraculous Candidate'). And then sometimes I can't come up with a good title at all!

INT: How does it feel when novels such as *Cal* and *Lamb* are filmed, and you write a screenplay as a member of a creative team?

BM: It's a different job and one that I enjoy. I've written a screenplay for a very fine novel by Robin Jenkins I read years ago called *The Cone Gatherers*, and we're currently trying to raise the money to film it. I've also written a screenplay for a fifteen-minute film, which I hope to direct in Ireland. It's loosely based on a poem, 'Bye-Child', by Seamus Heaney. My version is about some boys playing hide and seek and the grim discovery they make in an outhouse. It's also about one family's dark secrets – and how the blight of abuse can be passed from one generation to the next.

What's different about working in film is that you're part of a team. It begins with a producer, who believes he has found a good story and gets the writer involved. The next question is who will direct it? It's a pyramid structure: the more you go down the pyramid, the more people are involved in the creative process. There's a great camaraderie of the circus coming together for an intense ten days or eight weeks or whatever the time it takes to shoot the film – and there's a whole new process after that. You think you've got the story on film, and then you realise that the editing room is where you could make ten films, each of them different. For me it represents a whole new trade, and a very interesting one. This is my first time directing. It'll be a new bowel-churning experience for me! At the age of sixty I'm going to be in charge of thirty-seven professional people, telling them what to do! I presume if you get a good director of photography he will look after the lighting and all I will have to do is talk to actors about their performances. Oh and have a clear and focused idea inside my head of how it should all come together.

INT: Where is this film set?

BM: In the North of Ireland – at a remote farmhouse. We've discarded the poem itself, although it's a wonderful poem, because I don't think poetry works on film.

INT: You've also had the experience of your own novels being turned into films, haven't you? When her first novel, *Union Street*, was filmed Pat Barker said that the best of the story was left on the cutting-room floor; whereas you have had a much more positive experience. Do you think that's because you've been very involved in the film-making process?

BM: Yes – and I try to keep the screenplay as close to the book as possible – as long as it works on film. I have sacrificed certain things, like the opening sentence of *Lamb*, which is impossible to put on screen: 'There were things at the bottom of Brother Sebastian's bag that he didn't know were there.' You just can't *do* that on film. If you use an image you have to abandon everything that's word-based; for example, if you say, 'the brothers walked across the quad, their soutanes flapping like old crows', and you photograph that and then put in a shot of an old crow, it becomes nonsense!

INT: You talk about things that are lost, like the interiority of characters such as Brother Sebastian in that first sentence. But what do you think is gained when novels such as *Cal* or *Lamb* are transferred to screen?

BM: What is gained is the intensification of the emotion and the intensity of the story. An actor can communicate with an eyebrow what fiction might communicate slowly over several chapters. And then there's the music, like in that remarkable movie John Huston made of James Joyce's story, 'The Dead'. When the old woman, Aunt Julia, sings 'Arrayed for the Bridal', you just want to weep. And there's also the song of 'The Lass of Aughrim', an emotional linchpin, which is so important for Gabriel and Gretta. In films, the performance of the actors is also a significant gain. I've worked with excellent actors: Helen Mirren and John Lynch, Liam Neeson and Hugh O'Connor, the wee boy I thought was so remarkable in *Lamb*, who has now become a successful adult actor.

INT: What about perspective? In a novel like *Cal* the reader's perspective on events is very different from that which is transferred to the screen; like the scene in the film in which Cal and Skeffington meet, and there are overhead crane shots, and oblique angled shots, creating a perspective we don't have in the novel. Did that open up anything different for you in terms of viewing a version of your own writing?

BM: You write a screenplay, hand it over, and go on the set for the bacon rolls. Then when you see the first rough cut, you're truly astonished, and wonder where it all went, there's so much of it missing. The director has seen it his way, which you didn't imagine, and that is the collaborative element. There's got to be give and take. You can't flounce out and say, 'No, that's completely wrong', or 'That shot doesn't come over'. The director, you, the producer, everybody, are all making the same film. It's a different career, and it's one that I like, though I'm not so sure I quite like the idea of directing yet. But taking a novel, an original idea, and making images out of it, telling the story in a different way, I find fascinating. Of course, I've loved the cinema since I was a little boy. My father worked as advertising manager in the Capitol Cinema in Belfast, painting big signs like '*Coming Next Week*'. The signs were huge. He was a lettering expert. Do you remember '*Plus Full Supporting Programme*'?

INT: As well as working in film, you seem to divide yourself unusually evenly between novels and short stories. Do you see them as completely different arts, or are short stories something you do between novels?

BM: Flannery O'Connor talks about 'fictions of a certain length'. I would apply the same kind of principles to the novel as to the short story. There is a notion that a novel is something that you can relax into and have diversions from and live with, *feeling* the novel for a while; but I see the writing of short stories as just as important as writing a novel. I like Sean O'Faolain's saying: that the difference between the short story and the novel is the difference between a jumbo jet and a hot-air balloon. The jumbo jet is huge, like the novel. It can carry a vast number of passengers and takes a long time to get up in the air; whereas a hot-air balloon takes off immediately. It can only carry one or two people, but it can reach vast heights. They are differently marketed, though. If you say to a publisher, 'Well, I want to write a book of short stories', he'll choke back his ire and say, 'OK, we'll do those.'

INT: It's not until *The Anatomy School* that you seem to use humour in a sustained way – although, of course, there are brazenly humorous moments in 'Phonefun Limited' and other stories. Do you find that you first need a good joke or a good line?

BM: I now see comedy as part of the way people talk and the way they construct their sentences. What I was trying to do in *The Anatomy School* was to show the boys going through adolescence, and exploring the world through science, theology and sex, while the old people who are set in their ways are doing the same thing but in a different way.

Mary Lawless claims to have had a twenty-inch waist the day she was married. 'You had an elastic measuring tape, as well, if you ask me,' says Nurse Gilliland. And Mary Lawless is thinking about getting two sets of scales, one for each foot. Then what would she weigh? And there's religious knowledge: Father Farquharson's 'sacerdotal intentionality', the same absolutely mad theology that the boys go through in class. There's a comic plot with the elders while the boys explore similar ideas at a more serious level.

I suppose it's also my admiration for Flann O'Brien's *At Swim-Two-Birds*. In it there's conversations between Shanahan and Mr Lamont and Mrs Furriskey at the tea table, and it makes me howl with laughter every time I read it, because of its meandering nature. They begin discussing the human voice, move on to musical instruments – 'a fiddle is an awkward class of a thing to carry' – and Nero, and then to 'cures for blackheads', and then how a bad knee is a terrible thing: 'I knew a man got a crack of a door-knob on his knee.' 'Oh, come here now. How high was he?' It goes on for page after page after page. And bad blood is at the back of the whole thing – the nation's blood is poor. So I'm pinching from an Irish literary tradition I know and love. In some ways I am a very traditional writer.

Select criticism

Brienzo, Gary. 'The Voice of Despair in Ireland's Bernard Mac Laverty', *North Dakota Quarterly* 57: 1 (1989), pp. 67–77.

Calahan, James M. *Double Visions: Women and Men in Modern and Contemporary Irish Fiction* (Syracuse, NY: Syracuse University Press, 1999).

Kelly, Thomas. '*Secrets and Other Stories* by Bernard Mac Laverty', *Eire Ireland: A Journal of Irish Studies* 16: 1 (1981), pp. 155–8.

Saxton, Arnold. 'An Introduction to the Stories of Bernard MacLaverty', *Journal of the Short Story in English* 8 (1988), pp. 113–23.

Simpson, Paul and Martin Montgomery. 'Language, Literature and Film: The Stylistics of Bernarad Mac Laverty's *Cal*', in Peter Verdonk and Jean Jacques Weber, eds, *Twentieth Century Fiction: From Text to Context*. London: Routledge, 1995.

Stine, Jean C. and Daniel G. Marowski, eds. 'Bernard MacLaverty', *Contemporary Literary Criticism*, 31 (1985), pp. 252–7.

Watt, Stephen. 'The Politics of Bernard Mac Laverty's *Cal*', *Eire Ireland: A Journal of Irish Studies* 28: 3 (1993), pp. 130–46.

7 Michèle Roberts

Jenny Newman

Michèle Roberts, widely known for her luscious, energetic prose, defines herself as a modernist, and the fractured, inventive narratives of her early novels established her straight away as one of a new generation of feminist writers. In *The Book of Mrs Noah* (1987) Roberts addresses a major project of the women's movement: the recovery of a female tradition of writers, saints and mystics. Five storytelling sibyls from past and present float in an imaginary ark on the Venetian lagoon, listened to by a caricature God the Father, renamed the Gaffer, the first of several men in Roberts's fiction who are both drawn to and prey on creative women. Like the later *Flesh and Blood* (1994) and *Impossible Saints* (1997), this playful, challenging novel is a darkly comic set of stories within stories, and a passionate meditation on the nature of women's writing.

Women's stories are also central to Roberts's *Daughters of the House* (1992), which was shortlisted for the Booker Prize and won the 1993 W. H. Smith Literary Award. Structured as a list of household objects, this formally experimental novel probes the troubled French legacy of Occupation and Resistance and, like much of Roberts's work, gives a voice to an 'unofficial' historian – in this case a small girl, one of two contrasting sisters who inadvertently reveal a village's shameful secret.

While retaining a strong sense of the primacy of the writer over the critic, Roberts draws on psychoanalytic, linguistic and feminist theory. In particular she investigates mother–daughter relationships, sibling rivalry and – through the story of the fictitious St Josephine in *Impossible Saints* – the taboo love between father and daughter. Male writers in later novels such as *Fair Exchange* (1999) and *The Looking Glass* (2000) are allowed more creativity and complexity than the Gaffer; but it is the female characters who – like the maid Geneviève in *The Looking Glass* – remain the tellers of the central stories. In *The Mistressclass* (2003), Roberts delivers her most pressing account to date of both reading and writing: the story of Charlotte Brontë's passion for both is paralleled by that of the modern-day poet, Vinnie.

Roberts explores what it means to be painfully divided – from a sister, a mother (or mother figure) and from one's mother tongue. Half-English, half-French, Roberts looks back to Colette and George Sand, and her sibyls and female saints are sensuous rather than ascetic. Roberts's fiction celebrates colour, physical pleasure, mouth-watering food and sexual love, all of which she feels were dismissed and devalued during her Catholic schooldays.

Key works

■ Novels

A Piece of the Night. London: Women's Press, 1978.
The Visitation. London: Women's Press, 1983.
The Wild Girl. London: Methuen, 1984.
The Book of Mrs Noah. London: Methuen, 1987.
In the Red Kitchen. London: Methuen, 1990.
Daughters of the House. London: Virago, 1992.
Flesh and Blood. London: Virago, 1994.
Impossible Saints. London: Little, Brown, 1997.
Fair Exchange. London: Little, Brown, 1999.
The Looking Glass. London: Little, Brown, 2000.
The Mistressclass. London: Little, Brown, 2003.

■ Short stories

During Mother's Absence. London: Virago, 1993.
Playing Sardines. London: Virago, 2001.
Co-authored with Zoë Fairbairns, Sara Maitland, Valerie Miner and
   Michelene Wander:
Tales I Tell My Mother. London: The Journeyman Press, 1978.
More Tales I Tell My Mother. London: The Journeyman Press, 1987.

INT: You wrote at the end of your first novel, *A Piece of the Night*, that we carry the memory of our childhood like a photograph in a locket. Why does the past continue to inspire you?

MR: Probably for Freudian reasons. When you're young, you're open to the world, vulnerable, soft-shelled. I think your childhood stamps you, wounds you, shapes you. And then I think you struggle to turn it into language and make something of it. You may not have to be an artist to do that, but I've chosen to be inspired by the past.

   I think the fact that Mnemosyne, memory, is the mother of the muses is not an accident. The older I get, the more I think memory and creativity, memory and invention, are deeply connected. We would say to invent is to make up, but if you look at the Latin, *invenio* means 'I come upon, I find'. To make something up means to discover it. Perhaps it's always been there, but your process of discovering it means a novel.

My parents, for example, lived through the Second World War, and I got to the point where I needed to know what the war had been like for them – the truth for them of being young people before having us children. And then those parents stand in for all the people in history whom I've never met but want to know about. There's a political angle, too, which is about women or other 'lost voices', people who've been written out of history. I'm interested in trying to find and invent voices and stories of people who haven't been seen as important. And I think that makes me a late twentieth-century writer, because it's a project that lots of people have been involved with.

INT: In a lecture on 'The Place of Imagination' in 1994 you spoke about your urge to recreate childhood as a happy paradise. Do you feel that urge still prevails?

MR: Because that state never existed, I still want to get back to it. I don't think my childhood was terribly happy – no one's fault, one knows that now – but I felt very separate from my mother, much too separate: she was the paradise from which I had been 'expelled untimely'. The image of the maternal body as paradise became very important to me. Obviously it's there in psychoanalytical literature, but it was my journey to discover it.

I suppose it's a religious or mystical feeling or quest: to get back to some pre-linguistic state of bliss, which is about unity, non-separation. I would have thought that the baby at the breast is probably experiencing bliss similar to that which the mystic adult feels when reconnected with God and the universe. I don't feel that it's a put-down of that experience to say that childhood bliss is somewhere involved. I think childhood is a mythical state as much as a real one, and I'm interested in exploring myths, like that of Adam and Eve which is clearly about childhood and gender division but also a sort of personal search. It's *reculer pour mieux sauter.* You go back into the mythical past, the Golden Age, you get nourishment from some magical stream, you meet some magical beast, you might even reunite with this mother-goddess person, and then you're born again. You can start your life again. I think I periodically need to go back, bathe in that stream, and then leave again. It's not that I'd ever stay there – I probably wouldn't want to – it would probably be a state of psychosis, if you stayed in it!

INT: Does your vision of the child's state of bliss at the mother's breast affect the way you use language?

MR: In nearly everything I've written there are moments when characters experience a loss of ego and become enraptured. I've put it in a specifically religious context, as when I wrote about Mary Magdalene; I connected it with sexuality, but it's very much about her finding her voice as a prophet, a poet, a lover. I wrote about it in my version of St Teresa of Avila, Josephine, an 'impossible saint'. Doesn't Kristeva label the 'semiotic', which men and women can both have recourse to, as the 'blissful babble'? I think it also means that I compose visual images in my novels, and that in several of them the vision that somebody might have isn't just a vision of God or Christ. It's a vision of something I can see in my mind now; it's sort of golden, and it's a daughter and a mother who are joined. When you've had that vision, you are strengthened, you are able to live, you're able to not die. And I didn't always know that's what my characters were looking for. Sometimes I've not let on that it's there, as in *Impossible Saints*, where a male figure is present in a sort of trinity because that was me being somehow correct, that Josephine could somehow love both her parents. Actually, I think that my characters are looking for the mother, and it's golden. I didn't really understand that until I'd written six novels or so. So it's partly a linguistic style but it's partly the composition of a visual image in language.

INT: Do you think that your image of bliss is also part impulse to describe a new way of life, be it writerly or religious – like the one in *Impossible Saints*?

MR: I think the point about having an image of a mystical experience rooted in the body was my way of overcoming the Catholic split between body and soul which damaged me almost irreparably, I would say, as a young woman growing up, because it made me feel so bad about desire, sex, pleasure, myself, my own body. Part of what my work's been trying to do is to repair damage. The culture is damaged by that split, which still goes on. If you use the image of a convent, or a mystical quest, it's a way of giving yourself time to pause and access realities which aren't simply to do with the hustle and bustle of 'gotta make money, gotta rush about being sociable', the hurly-burly of the modern world, which I quite like; but it's very important that you try and create these little spaces which are slightly separate from normal daily time.

It's not that I'm a goddess worshipper, heaven forfend: I loathe all that sentimental kitsch. But if you go into this place that might be like a cave in your imagination – and that's where you go when you're writing a novel anyway – there might be something else shining at the back of the cave. I don't particularly want to say, 'It's this golden statue of a mother and a daughter', because that's too obvious. But the fact that there's something shining in the darkness is what draws me in. I think it's true of lots of those late nineteenth-century visionary experiences when children saw the goddess of the countryside, and then the Church wrestled it into shape and said, 'It's the Immaculate Conception', because they wanted that dogma promoted. So my little shining thing at the back of the cave is something similar.

INT: Your first novel begins with an image of a dead nun in the school chapel; and at the heart of *Daughters of the House* is Léonie's vision of the gold and red woman.

MR: I think that every novel I've written has come from an image, usually an image in a dream, that's been so powerful that I'm haunted by it or obsessed with it, and have got to translate the image into words, which means some kind of narrative. I've begun to see that often the vision is of a dead person, a dead woman, which is a bit horrible in a way, or a bit weird. The work of the novel, therefore, is to breathe life into this corpse. The corpse can sit up and talk, or is allowed to be resurrected in some way. I can see in a psychoanalytical sense – though that might be too narrow to use on its own – that a child might be very angry with her mother. 'I wish you were dead! I want to kill you – I hate you so much!' And then you've got this dead mother. The child's next move – this is Melanie Klein stuff – is to make reparation. You're sorrowful, you're guilty, you want to make Mamma better. And that is the impulse for art, some psychoanalysts believe. So I can see that there's something of that going on for me. In my new novel [*The Mistressclass*] I thought, 'I can't believe it, there's a bloody corpse in the opening chapter again!'

Death is the great fact of our lives, and some people think that artists create in order to deny it, deny their own death, so that your work of art becomes almost like a fetish. It's going to live on, you hope, it's going to have eternal life, though you might happen to be in the ground. I think actually that you make art in the teeth of death, facing it, with your eyes open, and you become fascinated by it. I am. I mean, what is a dead body? What does death involve? What are the physical processes? How can you know the people of the past, who are all dead? In what sense could you ever discover what it was like to be them? And I have come to realise very recently – this is neurotic, I think! – that that curiosity to know the dead is an image to me of what it means to know another person. I feel now that I walk in a world peopled by ghosts, and I write about ghosts very directly in my new novel. Partly it's melodrama and gothic, and partly it's just like reality. When you walk in this part of London, in the City, you feel these layers and layers of history. So the dead are everywhere around you. I think part of my fiction is saying, 'What is a relationship? What is it to be an "other"? Are we all the same? Are we one? Are we separate?' It's connected with the fact that I'm a twin. Part of my childhood inspiration was, 'What does it mean to look at somebody who is my twin, my double, my other? How do I know that I'm me and not her?' That used to terrify me when I was a child.

INT: You've written a lot about the pleasure you take in reading, starting with childhood books such as *The Black Riders* by Violet Needham.

MR: That's the magic about reading: you create visionary worlds inside yourself because the author is doing it, but somehow telling you to do it too, you've got to do it together. And I was lucky to live in a house with books in it. Both my parents read and my English grandmother read. She was an uneducated woman whom I just adored. She was my salvation goddess-person – very down to earth, very funny, very honest. And she read voraciously, so it was quite normal to read a lot. And Nana also made up stories and poems, so she taught me by example that you could invent things, you could create things in language. She was a very powerful example.

I loved the tales of the Round Table, and in particular the tragic love stories like that of Tristan and Isolde. I did like having my heart broken. We also had these books of folk tales – there were a couple of Sufi stories that I was enchanted by. There was one about a king to whom huge adventures happen and hundreds of years pass, but actually he's been sitting on a horse and he's just blinked. I suppose it was through those folk stories from India, in particular, that I learnt about magic and magical realism.

I read *Lolita* when I was only ten and had a very strong sexual response to it; it was the first time I can remember having sexual feelings of any kind, but so powerful, it was quite disturbing. I thought I was ill, or something – I think because I was very in love with my dad. And I read a lot of poetry – in adolescence you find poetry very easy to dive into. I loved John Donne and Gerard Manley Hopkins. There weren't many women poets around that I knew of – you just didn't get given women writers in those days. It wasn't until I went to university that I got access.

When I became a feminist in 1968, I felt that I'd come home. Although a lot of people now think of it as puritanical, narrow-minded, man-hating, for us it was about street theatre, talking joyfully about sex, having as much sex as you possibly could, drugs and music and all of that, and this passion for reading was part of it, searching for women authors. Virago and The Women's Press had just been founded, so women writers were flooding on to the market. It was a heady time.

I know that a lot of people now scoff at Virginia Woolf's idea of thinking back through our mothers, and the critic Lorna Sage, for example, got very fed up with the idea of a female literary tradition. She wanted there to be a community, now, of living writers. Well, of course – that's what we want; but I don't care how pathetic or insecure it makes me sound: I need to feel there are women writers at my back who are inspiring me. And they are, of course, versions of those saints I loved as a child. And I realise that most of those saints I loved were writers.

INT: Does it make you angry to be described as a woman writer or feminist writer?

MR: When you just say 'writer' it's nearly always been signed, unconsciously, as a man. And then you have 'woman writer' or 'black writer' or 'working-class writer' – 'the other'. And of course if you're put in that category of 'other' you're going to resent it. I think that's why so many writers I admire and esteem who are women did not wish to be called women writers, had no interest in feminism and didn't want to be in women-only anthologies. But I think they ended up accepting the status quo, which meant they had to somehow become a bit masculine. I prefer to tackle the issue head-on and say the world is riven by gender division. So I'm quite happy to say I'm a woman writer, though I don't believe in some kind of essentialist notion that by virtue of being a woman you automatically write differently to a man. I feel that denies writerly strategies, writerly sophistication and writerly choices, because there's a certain kind of good, old-fashioned, omniscient narrator that someone of either gender could write. Not all women write in a Kristevan, semiotic way.

INT: You say in your volume of essays, *Food, Sex & God*, that form is everything to writing, and that the demands of the subject help you create a form. How would you describe your preferred narrative structures?

MR: Every novel represents a new problem to be solved, and therefore you have to find and invent a new form. It's ambition: I want to play, I want to make something. I can now see that I have very personal reasons for distrusting older forms, and that they pushed me into being a modernist, breaking the old forms, wanting to make new ones. The personal reasons were to do with childhood, with the way my father in particular used language very powerfully and put me into his story. He was like God the Father on a cloud, the omniscient narrator, and I as a young girl, with very sexual feelings, felt trapped in his story of who I was in his life. I didn't know this for many years – I just had to flee from that kind of story, and preferred to invent new forms of the novel in which you might have several voices telling a story because they make a quarrel: voices not from up high looking down, but on the ground, or coming in from tangents, or narrative voices from the weak and the dispossessed, like in *Daughters of the House*. To me it's important that there are two little girls telling a story about history because I think the idea of a historian being a small girl is not one our culture believes in.

In *A Piece of the Night* I was asking, 'What is a woman?' It was about feeling fragmented and broken up – a mess on the carpet – and the narrative is fragmented too, because it moves according to memory. With *The Visitation* I was asking, 'How do men and women love each other? Can they really love each other?' Probably most people reading that novel wouldn't see that I've taken the structure of certain parts of the Bible and played around with them a bit. A novel which asks, 'Can you be both holy and sexual?' becomes recast as a gospel that's never been read. I'm not saying I'm finding earth-shattering solutions, but I am interested in making the novel different every time. Not just for intellectual reasons; it's an organic feeling – like if you had a baby, every one would look different. You wouldn't want to just have clones!

INT: When you described the process of writing *The Looking Glass* you spoke about how its narrative structure evolved into an exploration of the women's experience and also of the character of the poet.

MR: Male poets have been so central I thought that this one could be like the hole in the Polo mint. The women could all circle around him, inventing him, making him up and fantasising about him, because they're all sort of in love with him. I like the fact that you never see his poetry. In *Possession* A. S. Byatt did it brilliantly, and gave her two poets lots of room to have their poems in the text. I wanted to be more suggestive, so that you could guess what kind of poetry he'd write. It wasn't anti-the-man, it's just that the story of male power is told a lot. They're there in the culture, striding like giants.

INT: *The Looking Glass*, like so many of your novels, describes a woman in what you might call an altered state: when Geneviève finds herself in the church built over a plague pit in Rouen. Does that alarming 'other space' link with the blissful space?

MR: They are back to back. One's about a happy experience and the other's about trauma. I had mystical experiences as a child and then as an adolescent I also experienced terrors and emotional trauma which I thought meant I was mad, particularly as my family said I was. I feel I know about the kind of emotional distress that is frightening simply because you're not used to it. You feel you must be an outcast, alien, mad person. Now I think that most madness is extreme distress, extreme suffering, and if you can learn to contain it or make something with it, it helps you to cope with it. Art is part of that. I think it's part of being a writer that you go up and down a lot. There are days of such extreme despair. It's more despair than terror, but terror too! I now know what I've got to do which is go and do some writing, put a form on it. So poor Geneviève there . . . I made it up, that's never happened to me exactly, but I felt that I knew what she was about.

INT: The mermaid story is also about trauma and separation.

MR: And about sexuality. She is that Jungian mermaid of the unconscious, but she's also something between the mother and the daughter. Your reading is deep and beautiful, because you've thought so much about issues to do with women and women's creativity, so you bring that with you when you read things. And this will sound terribly arrogant, but I feel my books have somehow not always been properly read because they're talking about things that not everybody has thought about or wants to think about. I don't want to lay it out like a lesson because that's like a preaching text. But I think that's why you can feel so moved when you are read as you dream of being read. So thank you. Please put that in, that I said that!

INT: You write about everything from the Desert Fathers to the medieval mystics to nineteenth-century poets to the Nazis to the Bible. How far do you depend on research?

MR: Whatever else I'm doing in my life, I always read for several hours a day. And research: sometimes it's in order to get things right, like for *The Daughters of the House* I read a great deal about the Nazi occupation of France, because although I was relying partly on stories in the family, they're very mythical. A lot of the research never went anywhere near the novel, but I needed to do it to make me feel OK. The same with *The Wild Girl*: I read enormous amounts of Patristic literature, Gnostic texts and commentaries, and histories; and though they fell away, they fed me. When you are doing the research you find that everything's linked to everything else in a very crystalline way. That's what's underneath every novel, the world of the unconscious, which is a library as well. The reading doesn't necessarily show, but it's there and you keep going back into it. The unconscious is part of yourself: it's like this big country which sends you messages if you tune in and do your work.

INT: Is that where you feel that a novel is born, in the unconscious?

MR: The first year of a novel is frightening, because it's about getting lost. It's a serious madness, it really is; you feel you've somehow disintegrated and will never come back. But you've got to go there because otherwise you couldn't make anything new. That's why when I teach creative writing I get people to do automatic writing. I tell them we won't go past a few minutes, so they know there's some sort of line around it.

INT: Would you say that your novels are also born out of critical theory?

MR: I've just finished a reading of *Villette* which, because it uses images of maternity in the imagination, reveals a new *Villette*. So critical theory can engage with a text, and help you read more richly, more fully. And also it helps you see things you didn't see before, so there's a very positive, joyful, fertile side to it. But I do loathe the kind of critical theory which appears to obliterate works of art, and I use old-fashioned terms like 'works of art' deliberately, because a lot of work goes into a novel and the author does have a sense of what she's up to; so I resent the sort of readings which say the critic is everything. We have to give power back to the reader, yes, but when the writer is given no power I get cross.

On the other hand, it's good that we've had to question the canon and revalue our judgements. I've been part of a generation of readers who've joined the academics, and supported you and your battles, and feel grateful for what we've received, because my work is read sensitively by people who've thought a lot about those issues of critical theory and gender. It's like fresh air blowing around, with lots of notions about writers and difference being celebrated.

About fifteen years ago I went to a seminar in Germany on feminist critical theory, and Rachel Bowlby read a paper on the questioning, aggressive, demanding reader. She made me see that although there's an experience of reading that I love, which is being enraptured, seduced and carried away, there's another kind which is engaging with the text and having a real, equal-to-equal conversation. Sometimes that means hurling the book across the room! I once taught students with terrific difficulties in writing essays. What bogged them down was the reading of set texts and critical texts. I taught them that when you got to a bit that was boring or you didn't understand you skipped over it and kept going.

INT: How do you see your work now, in the middle of your career?

MR: You always try to make something better this time than you've done before. A Spanish critic pointed out that my books fall into groups, and I can see that they're to do with my own life and growing-up process. Up until the moment when I met my husband there was a lot of angry stuff and a fierce method of writing which was quite modernist and 'Fuck you if you want conventional stories, you're not getting them from me, and if I want to write about Catholicism I'll write about it and if I want to do it I'll do it and OK, I'm an outcast, an exile and a barbarian but I'm making the art I like!'

All my novels had been about homeless women, and then for the first time in my life I began to have a happy relationship with a man – no accident he's an artist – and I wrote *In the Red Kitchen*. It wasn't that men were suddenly heroes, it was more about human warmth. I felt I had a home, that imaginary space of warmth, and it had an effect on my writing. Next came *Daughters of the House* and *Flesh and Blood*, and then I wrote *Impossible Saints*. In that I laid a ghost, which was my terrible fear that my father and I had loved each other much too much. What came next was more playful, somehow, writing *Fair Exchange* and thinking, 'I want to look at feminine genres, I'll write a romance, I'll lark about.'

I now see that my novels have all had muses. The figure of the mother, an absent mother, was the muse for my first group. Then my husband was a muse for a couple of novels. My dad was a muse for *Impossible Saints,* and my neighbour in France, Mme Drouard, whom I love very much, has been the female muse for my last three novels. My French publisher, a man, suggested I write about William Wordsworth's love affair with Annette Vallon, which I did in *Fair Exchange.* So he was a muse for that book. A muse can be an imaginary figure, or a dead person, such as a saint, or a writer. Flaubert and Mallarmé have both inspired me, for example. George Sand too. Also, recently, Charlotte Brontë. So the muse becomes a subject as well as an inspiration.

INT: Does the idea of someone to whom you're writing make the activity less lonely?

MR: When Flaubert wrote to Louise Colet, his lover who lived in Paris, he would call her 'Dear Muse, Darling Muse'. And though he was sometimes horrible to her and kept her at this huge distance, he respected her brain. He sometimes seems to be a misogynistic, crusty old bastard, but to Louise he writes these amazing letters about writing *Madame Bovary*. Virginia Woolf said that everyone yearns for this perfect, beautiful critic and it's the same thing – the perfect reader. You're hoping someone will understand and like it, and say, 'It's beautiful.'

There's a sense that a book is a fantasy object, a fantasy of a gift, and it's offered to a fantasy reader, a fantasy muse. That's why, if you get a good review, it's not just narcissistic pleasure, it's a deeper thing, that you've been received, you've been somehow held, touched by the reader. And then of course you get readers reading your book in ways you don't expect at all, so they are very active and powerful. I've begun to see that what I would call a good book is one which allows that to happen, which doesn't beat the reader over the head and say, 'You've got to read it this way because I'm telling you to'. It's best to write in a way which frees the reader, if you can, to read it how she wants, and with luck she'll tell you what she's seen in it and you'll think, 'Oh, right! I didn't know I'd written that.'

INT: Do you feel that as a novelist you took on what we would call genre fiction, like the gothic, the love story, the detective story, the thriller?

MR: It's quite hard for women novelists because there are the very high literary figures such as Muriel Spark, Iris Murdoch, Doris Lessing and A. S. Byatt. Then there's middle-of-the-road, domestic realism. And then there's a lot of genre fiction, as though genre enables us to write about feminine or female concerns in a way that the model of what I call the male literary novel doesn't. We've certainly, historically, been readers of it. Like women read romances, men don't. A lot of thrillers are romances in disguise, and a lot of women who would have been writing romances thirty years ago are now writing thrillers. I loathe them, actually, because it's always about how Mr Right appears and he's a policeman – not what I'd call a thriller. But genre is connected to femininity in some weird way. For instance, the gothic allows you to dramatise issues around the body. I mean, the haunted house is a body, a maternal body, a sexual body, a dead body.

Literary theory has questioned the distinction between high art and low art and why genre fiction is worse than what's called the literary. Not that we've answered those questions, but because they're being asked in public it means you can feel more comfortable about moving between genres. Jacqueline Rose argues that one reason why Sylvia Plath makes people cross is that she moves across genres. She was writing stories for *Mademoiselle* while writing stories like 'Johnny Panic and the Bible of Dreams', which was much more literary and strange. She resisted being pigeon-holed, and I found that a very empowering part of Jacqueline Rose's book [*The Haunting of Sylvia Plath*], because that's what I was deliberately doing in *Playing Sardines*. Some of the stories were written for radio, so there's got to be a narrative and you can't be too tricksy or poetic. I found it liberating, that you could just tell a tale – the constraint was 2,200 words – and then with the other stories in the volume you could play. I thought, well, I've always been interested in the ways that soft porn for women is marketed as romance. I don't find modern romances sexy, but I did in my youth. Novels by Georgette Heyer embodied my fantasies and longings around men. They also created them in quite damaging ways – the bloody hero, so able and wonderful. Because I was so marked by them I had to come back and deal with them – like with *Fair Exchange*. I always say it's my homage to Georgette Heyer.

INT: How do you see yourself in today's literary landscape?

MR: I've moved on from being some sort of barbarian exile in my own head. In 1992–3 I got shortlisted for the Booker Prize and won the W. H. Smith Literary Award for *Daughters of the House*, and became much more visible. I'm now connected to the establishment in various ways, and sit on various committees and judge various prizes, and the stakes get upped, I think. Because it's your occupation to write a better novel every time, you're much more aware of being watched, and of questions like, 'Can she do it again?' or, 'Has she done a boo-boo this time?' You just have to live with it. The positive side is that when you get older you do get more comfortable in your skin, with luck, which I think I am. When I was young I wanted to set the world alight, I wanted to be the greatest novelist in the whole of English literature, I wanted to change the world for women. Now I'm more accepting that I'm not Albert Camus, I'm not Simone de Beauvoir, I'm not Georges Sand or Flaubert, I'm Michèle Roberts plodding along doing my best!

INT: But your writing still has a moral purpose?

MR: In a post-Christian culture you have to think hard about what your morality is. Maybe it has something to do with ecology – looking at ways in which things are connected, like spaces in cities, or country and city, or people. I still believe that being as kind as you can is the hardest thing in the world; not being so egotistical that you fail to see what other people might need, and yet balancing that with your own needs. As a writer you're practising that every day.

I'm acutely aware of how cruel people are to children, and to me that goes on being a moral issue of great importance. An awful lot of wrongdoing in later life can be traced back to having been the recipient of cruelty. If you don't know that other people can regard you with tenderness, how do you learn to regard them with tenderness? You can't, mostly. And that, of course, you can learn from thrillers, if you read them sensitively. Modern thrillers, good ones, I think, write tenderly about what goes wrong, and why people end up doing awful things. That's a great issue in the world today: the way we split the world into the goodies and the baddies, and that's got its place in novels. But now I'd try to just put it in as part of the story, and trust that the reader is there with me, huddling over, asking, 'Why are these adults behaving so badly?' That's where a certain kind of realism helps, because you can have various characters with the pull and the sympathy, not just the young woman.

INT: Finally, what do you think about the state of the novel today?

MR: You can't help worrying that the novel's days are numbered in some sense because the myth – and perhaps it is a myth – is that young people don't read like people of my generation did. I don't worry so much about books as physical objects vanishing; if there's going to be little hand-held computerised versions, that's terrific, that's technology – although I'm not into it myself much. But sometimes you get a sense that in this culture novels aren't important.

Yet a lot of novels are getting published, literary prizes are booming, and writing and reading are flourishing. And there's an enormous variety of novels we can read, experiments and varieties of written English from all over the world. But commercially there's a problem, because writers are finding it increasingly hard to make a living. The loss of the Net Book Agreement means that certain kinds of books get pushed at the expense of others, and lots of small, independent bookshops have closed. That all worries me a lot, and I worry about writers not making a living. If you're not the kind of writer who can be marketed in five ways, then maybe you'll fall through the net. On the other hand there's the rise of writers' groups, and all the chat rooms on the internet, so at least for readers there might be ways around the over-commercialisation of literature. I just hope that we go on cherishing the unfashionable and the eccentric.

Select criticism

Luckhurst, Roger. '"Impossible Mourning" in Toni Morrison's *Beloved* and Michèle Roberts's *Daughters of the House'*, *Critique: Studies in Contemporary Fiction* 37: 4 (Summer 1996), pp. 243–60.

Neubert-Köpsel, Isolde. 'Deconstructing Duality: Utopian Thought in the Concept of "Gender Blending" in Michèle Roberts's *Flesh and Blood'*, in Beate Neumeier, ed., *Engendering Realism and Postmodernism*. Amsterdam: Rodopi, 2001.

Parker, Emma. 'From House to Home: A Kristevan Reading of Michèle Roberts's *Daughters of the House'*, *Critique: Studies in Contemporary Fiction* 41: 2 (Winter 2000), pp. 153–73.

Reitz, Bernhard. 'Virgins in the Frying-Pan: Peepholes and Perspectives in Michèle Roberts's *Daughters of the House'*, in Beate Neumeier, ed., *Engendering Realism and Postmodernism*. Amsterdam: Rodopi, 2001.

Rowland, Susan. 'Michèle Roberts's Virgins: Contesting Gender in Fictions. Re-writing Jungian Theory and Christian Myth', *Journal of Gender Studies* 8: 1 (1999), pp. 35–42.

Rowland, Susan. 'Women, Spiritualism and Depth Psychology in Michèle Roberts's Victorian Novel', in Susan Rowland and Juliet John, eds, *Rereading Victorian Fiction*. London: Palgrave, 2002.

Sceats, Sarah. 'Eating the Evidence: Women, Power and Food', in Sarah Sceats and Gail Cunningham, eds, *Image and Power: Women in Fiction in the Twentieth Century*. London: Longman, 1996.

Stowers, Cath. '"No Legitimate Place, No Land, No Fatherland": Communities of Women in the Fiction of Roberts and Winterson', *Critical Survey* 8: 1 (1996), pp. 69–79.

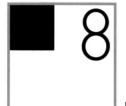

8 Barry Unsworth

David Evans and Jenny Newman

Barry Unsworth's literary career spans five decades, and his fourteen novels include *Sacred Hunger*, a joint Booker Prize winner in 1992, *Morality Play*, shortlisted for the Booker Prize in 1995, *Mooncranker's Gift*, which received the Heinemann award in 1973, and *Pascali's Island*, shortlisted for the Booker Prize in 1980 and subsequently filmed.

Though Unsworth takes a sharp and sometimes sardonic look at English provincial life, some of his greatest novels are set outside Britain and are clearly influenced by his fascination with the Eastern Mediterranean region. While still showing comic talent, his work has become increasingly capacious and profound, placing him among writers of international significance. The prize-winning *Sacred Hunger* explores the transatlantic slave trade in the mid-eighteenth century, using a range of viewpoints to dramatise not only the brutal treatment of the African captives but also the exploitation of the press-ganged white working-class crew of the slave ship. Unsworth's increasingly sharp moral curiosity and his search for a clear contemporary relevance raise his fiction high above the historical novel genre. Reviewers have compared him to both Joseph Conrad and William Golding (whose *Rites of Passage* pipped *Sacred Hunger* to the Booker Prize in 1980), while recognising the uniqueness of his gift for shifting from the cosmic to the comic even in his most serious works.

Unsworth describes himself as an 'old-fashioned romantic pessimist' in his attitude towards politics and society. His situations tend to be extreme, his flawed but usually sympathetic characters exposed to revelatory pressure and almost invariably troubled by guilt, obsession, vengefulness, sexual need or events beyond their control. His most recent novels also debunk heroism and heroics, whether 'historical' as in *Losing Nelson* (1999) or legendary as in *The Songs of the Kings* (2002).

Though pre-eminently concerned with strong storytelling, Unsworth is deeply conscious of craft and style, elements reflected throughout his novels in his loving treatment of activities as far apart as ship-building, restoring a sculpture, authorship, acting or the making of plaster pixies. Art, he implies in *Morality Play*, has a powerful social function: it is both truth-seeking and truth-telling in a world of lies, deceit and propaganda.

Key works

The Partnership. London: New Authors Ltd, 1966.

The Greeks Have a Word for It. London: Hutchinson, 1967.

The Hide. London: Gollancz, 1970.

Mooncranker's Gift. London: Allen Lane, 1973.

The Big Day. London: Michael Joseph, 1976.

Pascali's Island. London: Michael Joseph, 1980.

The Rage of the Vulture. London: Granada, 1982.

Stone Virgin. London: Hamish Hamilton, 1985.

Sugar and Rum. London: Hamish Hamilton, 1988.

Sacred Hunger. London: Hamish Hamilton, 1992.

Morality Play. London: Hamish Hamilton, 1995.

After Hannibal. London: Hamish Hamilton, 1996.

Losing Nelson. London: Hamish Hamilton, 1999.

The Songs of the Kings. London: Hamish Hamilton, 2002.

INT: You've lived abroad for most of your adult life, in Greece, Turkey, Finland and now Italy. To what extent has this shaped the kind of writer you've become?

BU: I spent my early childhood in a mining village in County Durham, a very close-knit community. Leaving there was a wrench which I still remember. Then my parents died when I was quite young, and this too was a sort of dislocation. Going to live in Greece in my twenties was simply one more uprooting, and with each subsequent uprooting the sense of home, of a familiar place, grew less and less. Now, in a certain way, I'm a stranger everywhere, and it suits me down to the ground. I think it's a good position for a novelist to have a sense of just passing through, of being a temporary visitor, and having the sort of licence and irresponsibility that goes with not belonging. The penalties are feeling too much on the surface of things, and not engaged sufficiently with life locally or anywhere else. But it's become such a habit with me now that I take it for granted. So I think living abroad was just one element in that process.

INT: Many of your novels – such as *The Songs of the Kings* and *Sugar and Rum* – incorporate a debate on literary technique. *Pascali's Island* in particular could be described as a meditation on what it means to be a novelist. Do you feel closer to Pascali than to your other main characters?

BU: Pascali identifies himself as both spy and creative artist. Like the
Singer in *The Songs of the Kings*, he has a sense of being poised at a
point of vantage, of being an observer, and that's part of the way I
look at the world too. In his report to his Turkish paymaster – the
novel takes the form of this report – Pascali invents the island all over
again, having started off fairly scrupulously recording the doings of the
Greek nationalists and revolutionaries. When he finds that his reports
are never acknowledged – because no reports were acknowledged in
this declining Ottoman empire – he turns to describing the island as it
might be, or as he thinks it should be. His bisexuality and diverse
religious sympathies – those things that divide him and make him
seem ambiguous – are also part of the distance he needs to register
experience and transmute it.

My conviction that the author too needs this kind of distance grew
stronger as I wrote *Pascali's Island*, and linked up with my idea, which
has also developed since, that the novelist, the fiction writer, the
storyteller, needs a sense of something urgent to impart, the pressure
of something felt personally and uniquely. It may not be original, but
it has to seem unique. Something like the telling of a secret,
something that needs to be told. But before that can be told, the
means of telling must be found, and that's always an experiment, a
pressure that remains through the experimental period of writing a
particular novel. In the case of *Pascali's Island*, the narrator is recording
his experiences from day to day, and the way he enters his fictional
world gives a strong element of immediacy to the text. There's this
shuttling between the world of transactions and negotiations and
experiences and back again, which I found technically interesting.
Pascali also has the novelist's irrepressible desire to see his works in
print. He wants to reach Constantinople and find connections, publish
his work in volume form and be an author. I don't think that I am
quite as ambiguous as Pascali is, but yes, he is an alter ego!

INT: Does the attention you pay to the process of writing a novel relate to
your love of craftsmanship, as expressed, for example, in your
description of the making of the garden figures in *The Partnership*, or of
the sacrificial knife in *The Songs of the Kings*, or of the restoration work
in *Stone Virgin*?

BU: In *Stone Virgin* the process of the restoration is a sort of device or way
of containing the action, limiting the narrative frame. The shape of the

story is determined and measured out by the stages of the restoration of the statue, which is at the beginning encrusted with the results of air pollution. Step by step, painstakingly, meticulously, it is being restored to something like its pristine form and surface. Where this ends is where the book ends, and the process also acts as a symbol of human restoration, of some degree of recovery, even redemption. So it does have a dual function. The same is true of the slave ship in *Sacred Hunger*; except that here the narrative takes us beyond the building of the ship to her subsequent voyage and final destination. The Liverpool I knew in the 1980s was a devastated city, but the Liverpool of the 1750s when the slave ship was built was in a phase of expansion, shortly to become a major Atlantic port; and the purpose of *The Liverpool Merchant* – to transport slaves – was regarded as right and proper because it was profitable. In *The Songs of the Kings* the making of the knife likewise serves to say something about technology and the ways in which it can justify everything, supplanting moral value or even moral perspective. Agamemnon's absorption in the knife supplants to a large degree the real nature of what he is about to do. It became a state of the art sacrificial knife!

INT: In general, how do you feel that such ideas are best conveyed to your reader?

BU: I can't imagine writing a novel without a strong element of the visual. My characters talk to each other, but they also register sights and sounds: the quality of the light, the nature of the shadow, the shape of the clouds, the rustling of the leaves. I think that in life, when we recall important experiences, they are accompanied by residual visual impressions, and for me that's important, though for other writers it may not be. It's not a necessary element of great fiction, but those writers that I admire and that have had an effect on me were all people who used visual effect in that way. I don't say I'm as good as they are, but to become part of that company of people who do those things was my first impetus as a writer. My earliest influence was Eudora Welty, when I picked up the Penguin edition of *A Curtain of Green*, introduced by Katherine Anne Porter. The title story has a murderous moment, where a white woman, Mrs Larkin, is in her garden looking down at the young black gardener who is kneeling among the plants with his back to her. It hasn't rained all day, and the air is full of the need for rain; and she has this moment where she could strike the boy with her hoe and kill him. It passes and the rain comes. A wonderful use of the visual intensifies the episode and makes some sort of statement about human experience that transcends the moment and becomes universal. So I tried to write like Eudora Welty for a while. But I was in Stockton-on-Tees and she was in Mississippi, and it didn't go down well as a combination! At least, the editors of the magazines I sent my stories to didn't think so, and my stories were returned. Later on, William Golding exemplified for me a wonderful use of visual effects, and Joseph Conrad and Graham Greene, in their different ways. They were all writers who knew how to convey the physicality of things.

INT: Some of your novels are written from a single point of view, and in others you shift it, sometimes paragraph by paragraph. Does point of view choose you or do you choose it?

BU: I test it out in my mind before I start: how it would sound written in the first person, or in a single third-person consciousness and voice, and how it would sound sort of shifting. I test it in relation to the story itself, how it would work best. It's instinct, really. There are snags and advantages in all of these forms. *Sacred Hunger* had such a big canvas, and so many characters, it was obvious that I would have to shift around, interpose reflections and comments, maintain a sort of moralising authorial voice in the tradition of nineteenth-century fiction. It seemed natural to use whatever narrator, whatever voice, was most convenient, most conducive. If you do it widely enough, it works very well, especially if there are various regions of the world involved.

With *Morality Play* that technique would not have worked at all. It's a detective story, so I couldn't give too much away. It seems that the books I write come out different shapes and sizes. Although there are similarities, they're often diverse in form and period, so I need to think pretty clearly about the way I'm going to write them. Until I've done that I can't do anything. It took me as long to find Pascali's voice as it did to write the novel. It felt very, very important to get the right idiom for the narration, to get the right focus, and that remains for me a tremendously significant thing.

INT: So each new novel presents you with a new technical challenge?

BU: Art is always about discovery, and the experience of writing a novel is also a process of self-discovery in the sense that I don't think one has any clear formulation at the outset. One needs the sense of a dynamic form to start a novel – you can't just put to sea without any sense of destination. For me, anyway, that sense of the basic dynamic is necessary. But the actual complex of feeling, the resolution, what the novel is actually about, would only come at a later stage. For me, that would mean discovering what I really felt.

In *Morality Play*, for instance, the play has a stage process and a verbal process. The plot's main discoveries are made by almost involuntary verbal formulations which seem to descend on the actors like a sort of grace. I felt that *Morality Play* was about that process of art towards discovery, and the sense of breaking down boundaries to reach some knowledge collectively that couldn't have otherwise been reached. In *Sacred Hunger* there is a community in the wilds of Florida composed of slaves and of the sailors who were dealing with them – all people who have the print of slavery on them and live in a violent age at the lowest end of the social scale. They try to found a Utopian community in which they would escape this print of slavery, and live in a society where the coercions of authority and the taint of trade would no longer exist. They would try to return to nature, which was an eighteenth-century preoccupation, the idea that man is by nature good. Whether they would succeed or not was a question for me as writer. It's something that emerges from the fiction, not something that's given to you: it's up for grabs, so to speak. You have to decide, well, what do you feel about that? Do you feel it would succeed or not? What sort of hope do you have for the human race? That is the meaning of the novel, and that is something I feel to be one of the most self-fulfilling things, this journey, this realisation, a sense of the truth that you arrive at.

INT: What governs your choice of tense?

BU: I generally dislike present-tense narrative, because I find it difficult to manage and in certain ways contrived-seeming. Though it's an unnatural form, the historic present, large numbers of novels these days are written in this tense and very often they don't succeed. To my mind they deny the novel one of its strengths, which is the sudden increase of tension that comes from the occasional use of the present. They denude the novel of that possibility by using it throughout.

I prefer to use the present occasionally, not pervasively, except when there is a dramatic need for it, as there was in *Pascali's Island*, where the narrator's time was running out and he was frantically recording, and beginning to understand who and what he was. I returned to this use of the present tense in one strand of *Stone Virgin*, where the fifteenth-century narrator is in prison. He too knows he's under sentence of death, and is desperately trying to enlist the aid of his patron. He has to stop writing whenever the jailer enters the cell, so there's a similar sense of urgency as he struggles with words and tries to shape them.

INT: In your early novel, *The Hide*, Audrey feels bereft partly because she is told she cannot play Mrs Alving in Ibsen's *Ghosts*. Then there is the pageant in *Sugar and Rum*, and *The Tempest* in *Sacred Hunger*. Why does the theatre feature so much in your work?

BU: It has a different function in every novel. Early on, in *The Big Day*, for instance, the fancy dress party was a sort of burlesque representation of what were caricatured personages. If *The Big Day* succeeds at all, it succeeds on the level of caricature. A lot of fiction set in the past is trying to strike a note which would seem to belong to that period, like the eighteenth-century interest in the possibilities of regeneration and Utopian redemption, and the illusion that through these theories you could improve on Shakespeare. The version of *The Tempest* in *Sacred Hunger* is an inferior version; but it deals with the noble savage and the fate of Caliban, and also the beginnings of colonialism. The slave trade wasn't itself colonial, but a softening-up process for colonialism. Having ruined the African economy, Europeans then decided that Africans needed help, and that the best way to help them was to go in there and take over. It's very hard to detach the play-acting from the general feeling of the period in *Sacred Hunger*.

The play in *Morality Play* is also part of the structure. A story that deals with the actors' attempts to discover the truth through their play had been in my mind for many years: the idea that travelling players could arrive at a place, perform a curtain-raiser to get the crowd in, and find themselves in difficulties because they'd come too near a truth. I shifted the narrative back to a time when the theatre was developing, a crucial point in its history, the transition from miracle plays to the morality plays which had a new emphasis on psychology and secular themes which led to the Renaissance and to theatre as it became.

INT: Do you also use the theatre to show up the awkwardness, physically and sexually, of some of your characters?

BU: Audrey in *The Big Day* and Erasmus in *Sacred Hunger* are both to some degree maladjusted. The rigidity of personality which prevents them from entering into the theatrical is perhaps a way of indicating, not necessarily faults of character, but characteristic qualities. It certainly was for Erasmus, who hated to be anything but himself. This partly explains his behaviour later in the novel. He becomes relentlessly focused on one single interpretation of events and one single solution because of his total lack of any play of mind.

INT: You recently remarked that you've never returned to the ethos or style of *Mooncranker's Gift*. Do you see that novel as a turning point?

BU: It marked a point of departure or transition. I have never returned to that density of prose or images, or that metaphoric content. When I was writing *Mooncranker's Gift* I was in love with language in a way that I still am, but not now with that degree of exuberance, that delight in the possibilities of image and cadence, and the exciting baroque element there is in the novel. It's one of the novels that stays in my mind as belonging to a particular time, and it stands alone among the books I've written. It was the first novel in which I used the past as an element in the fiction: the acropolis on the hillside, the ancient Greek city, the fallen columns, and so on. But that's not what I remember about it; it's more this feeling about language that filled my mind for two years.

INT: Would you describe yourself now as a historical novelist?

BU: I've always felt that the history is a pretext for morality, and look for something in the past that relates to the present. I think that one has to get the period right in order to be convincing, but if the definition of a historical novel is that its chief concern is to recreate a period, with all its colour and fascination, and that is its raison d'être, then in that case it remains genre fiction. I don't feel I've been writing genre fiction. I've been writing novels set in the past, with clear contemporary relevance. It's not only a question of historical research, it's a question of historical imagination: the nature of fighting at sea in the eighteenth century in *Losing Nelson*, the way the voices of the wind are described in *The Songs of the Kings*, and the way it blows through the wheat so that the whole field becomes yellow, almost the same tone as the tawny-coloured hills beyond. Even the smell of the latrines becomes part of the army's life. That's Ajax! That's the military mind! One thing I discovered about myself as I went on writing – round about the time of *Mooncranker's Gift* – was that whatever the shortcomings of my fiction, I have discovered a certain historical imagination, a sense of period, and I think somehow an authentic charge from the past. That's why I get so cross when my novels are done as screenplays, and the screenwriter has no sense of history. He just makes blunder after blunder, and this is offensive to me, like bad syntax.

INT: In *Sugar and Rum* you describe Benson as being every now and again 'ambushed by his past', because he had made a mistake in the Second World War which led to his friend's death. Mooncranker's gift of the sausage-meat Christ was an injury Farnaby carried into adulthood, and Raikes's past act of cowardice in *The Rage of the Vulture* continues to colour his present. What do you see as the link between past and present in the individual life?

BU: It's obvious that a moment of crucial importance which changes the colour and quality of somebody's life is a useful fictional device. When you can focus on something like that and talk about the result in a particular human life, it's hard then to make the transition and ask yourself if that's what you really think life does, as it is lived out there. It may be simply a romantic notion of destiny, of a fateful event. Many of Conrad's characters spend their time trying to expiate things that normally you might just want to forget! But this is essential to his fiction, and it seems it is essential to mine. If it results in some sort of truth being revealed, it seems to be justified in a certain sense. As a device, it's acceptable.

INT: Why do you push so many of your characters into extreme states: fear in *The Rage of the Vulture*, and desire and greed in *Sacred Hunger*, or even drunkenness in *Sugar and Rum*?

BU: Extremes work towards isolation, towards cutting people off from familiar backgrounds, familiar associations, to a stark sort of solitude of mind or being. I don't think these decisions have always been rational, just a way to get at what I'm hoping to get at. Writing a novel is an evasive process, that I'm sure of. Novelists are people who have something to hide. There are all sorts of other aspects to it that I haven't analysed and for my own self-preservation never will.

INT: How much do you revise and redraft?

BU: The only time I enjoy writing novels is at a certain intermediate stage – a third draft, really. I hate the first marks on the page, and struggle to get a rough draft which can bear the burden of being revised and expanded. My first drafts are sixty or seventy pages, always in pencil, and always written hastily with a strong sense of irresponsibility and haste and feeling of approximation. Then there is a second draft in which I try to expand, and that is hellish, because I come face to face with my own inadequacies and the inevitable failure of words to do justice to what I feel. So that's a suffering, and a tribulation that lasts some months, and I'm always pretty bad-tempered and edgy during that period. Then I come to a stage at which I've got perhaps a hundred and fifty or two hundred pages in ink, with corrections in red ink. I always use notebooks with wire backs, and write on one side and put notes on the other with asterisks. And then comes this really rather splendid third draft in which I incorporate the red ink and expand and contract and make associations more clear and emphatic, and shape it up and get it right as far as I can. I enjoy that, because it's a thing done. Then I transfer it to the computer, then see it in print and do revisions. And that's a whole different process, but also rather pleasurable. Once I get through these first two phases, I start feeling like a human being again and am able to be reasonably civil!

INT: Your fiction has always explored the nature of love, beginning with the homosexual Moss in *The Partnership*, who is willing to live with the narcissistic Foley without any physical sex because he believes that love is about feelings, not actions.

BU: Moss is an admirable character. He may not choose his times awfully well, and be clumsy in some of his dealings, but in moral terms he is far superior to Foley, whose love is fairly shallow and self-regarding. It's still a subject of debate: whether the giving of the self is a good thing or not; whether the guarding of the self is better than love, or whether the right balance can be found. That too would be a wonderful subject for a novel: how one tries to find the balance between self-giving and self-guarding. If you give too much you lose yourself, if you guard too much you've got nothing to give. I didn't know these things before I wrote *The Partnership*. Someone spoke to me when I was twenty years old in a way that no one had spoken to me before. It revealed a totally unsuspected aspect of this person, and this became the basis for whatever is in *Stone Virgin* about love, betrayal or readiness to self-sacrifice. In retrospect I think I could have made a much better novel of *The Partnership* if I'd known then what I think I know now.

INT: Do you feel that questions of sex and sexual relations remain central to your fiction?

BU: It may be to do with age and waning power, but I haven't dwelt so much on physical sexuality of late as I did in the earlier novels. In *Morality Play*, for instance, the sexual crime is meant to be held in abhorrence. But sexuality is obviously a determining factor in our relationships, and the relationship of sexuality to love is also interesting and important, the explicit lovemaking between a man and a woman. I dealt with that to some extent in *Stone Virgin*. The sickness of betrayal for Raikes is that a woman who he thought was responding to a feeling of deep attraction, the beginnings of love, was actually thinking of opportunities and expediencies. It was a use of sexuality that made him almost physically sick when he thought about it. I think that novel is about love, and the exploitation and corruption of love. Certainly through women: the way women are used and in return use back. It is what the Italians call quite an *intreccio* – an entanglement of love and desire.

INT: Do you see betrayal as one of your major themes?

BU: Betrayal and the misuse of power, and what it means to be a victim. Cleasby, in *Losing Nelson*, is a victim of his own hero-worship. Iphigenia, in *The Songs of the Kings*, is the quintessential victim. Some reviewers objected to my portrayal, in that she acquiesces in her fate, and this is not something that in our time the heroine is supposed to do. She is supposed to fight back, to be combative, so the book had to contend with that sort of reaction. Iphigenia is simply a pawn in a game and her collaboration is only required because that's less messy. It might be thought that there should be more sorrow for her fate, that there should be more tears in it. But the novel is not so much about what happens to Iphigenia, it's about what happens whenever this kind of collective enterprise is undertaken and runs into difficulties and needs to find pretexts. It's political, more than anything else, so the space for Iphigenia to react is limited, and so is the space in which she can register events, in the same way that her father, Agamemnon, has very limited space. Both are seen mainly from other people's points of view.

The translation of ancient myth into the direct action of modern fiction is hedged around with difficulties, partly because a novel, unlike an epic, has a naturalistic form. In the myth, Iphigenia was sent from Mycenae to Aulis. She could have turned up any time; as far as the myth is concerned she's just there. But the epic is a vanished form. In a novel, Iphigenia has to get a ship, time is needed, there are physical elements, the whole thing has to be spaced out. Also, there's no guilt in the epic, only shame; so in psychological terms the action of the novel has to be transformed. With Agamemnon, for example, you can accept the fact indirectly that he was ready to sacrifice his daughter, that he had thought of that, and that then his ambition was worked by very adroit and manipulative counsellors. That corresponds to our sense of what happens politically in our own time.

Why would one retell a story, unless to reflect some sense of our world through this transference of a sacrifice myth? I remember wondering, what would Agamemnon feel? I couldn't cope with it! Agamemnon never existed, he's a figure in a myth. My Agamemnon has to be something else. An indirect effect is necessary, a very stringent distancing. I can't translate the language of Aeschylus, who dealt very well with Agamemnon's feelings in the first play in the *Oresteia*, his trilogy, because his play could function as a direct register without any impediment. For me to deal directly with a father in the throes of deciding whether or not to sacrifice his daughter, and to deal with a daughter who finds herself betrayed by the father she trusted, would be to write another sort of novel, telling a story already told by Euripides in Athens in the fourth century BC.

Insofar as my novel is satirical, insofar as it's about political machinations, and insofar as it's really about people being moved around on a board, the direct intrusion of a father's intimate struggles – the clash between his desire to be a winner and giving up to death his beloved daughter – doesn't belong. Euripides did, I feel, though of course with reservations, the sort of thing I am trying to do now. He made use of that myth to say something about the Athenian state and its notions of heroism and responsibility. He was satirising a story which had been taken entirely seriously by Aeschylus, and writing in a different period of the Athenian progress towards the polis, towards statehood. The story of Iphigenia has been used again and again for one purpose or another, so I'm just one in a long line.

If I had to define myself, I would say I'm an old-fashioned romantic pessimist in my general attitude towards politics and society. It seems to me that I have tried to find themes that are not only universal, but just as true today. History is repeated again and again. Every time you look at eyewitness accounts, early versions, you find the same conflicts, the same lies, the same contradictions. This sense of history as being a synthesis of many points of view, none of which is totally trustworthy, is fascinating and complex. But it also relates the past to the present in a forceful way, and the past becomes simply a focus, a removal of contemporary clutter, which will isolate certain factors to help make that bridge. It is astonishing how little one needs to write about the past in order to convince the reader that it's an authentic picture. There's a common illusion that you have to pile detail upon detail, and you have to do all this research, but it isn't really true. You have to render certain significant things.

INT: Do you take your readers into account during the writing process?

BU: At some stage, yes; but I think expression comes before communication unless those two things are so closely intertwined that they are inseparable. Getting it right comes first, and when you are wrestling with getting it right you aren't really thinking about a reader. You're just thinking about doing justice to the poor, bare vision that you harbour. Some people have obviously read my work and liked it and I try to imagine these people. But they're so diverse in age and occupation that that too is difficult. I just think that my ideal reader would be a huge collective multitude!

INT: Do you have a muse?

BU: I've had a muse since Aira and I started living together. She's been my muse and my help and my point of departure, really, and my support. I write to please her first, and if it passes her I feel it's OK, so in that sense she has been my muse. Before that I didn't have a muse at all. I had all sorts of adventures with women, but I don't think that any of them were muses. Aira is an intensely serious person, and it's very important for her that one should say something that helps to some extent, if only minutely, not to change the world but to affect the way other people might see it. She has sharpened my conscience and my sense of responsibility, and I think she has taken me away from a rather narrowly defined provincial Englishness into what I feel to be the world, now, rather than a sort of island.

INT: Where do you see yourself in today's literary landscape?

BU: I don't really see myself anywhere there. If I defined myself as a writer I would belong to the tail-end of the realist–modernist movement of the first half of the twentieth century. That was a great period of the novel, and I think we are still living in its aftermath. I don't really relate to the postmodernist novel because I don't believe in authorial intrusion, I don't believe in letting the ragged edges show, I don't believe in clashes of discourse. Although I find that interesting in other writers, in a sense what has happened to the novel in the last thirty years is alien to me, except perhaps to the historical novel, for lack of any better terminology. The uses to which the past has been put is arguably the single most important development of the last quarter of the twentieth century. I feel I belong in some degree to a certain movement with a certain sense of the past, and a certain exploitation of the past in terms of metaphor. I feel I'm somewhere in there.

If I had to cite the two elements that seem to have been determinative for me, one would be moral curiosity, and the other an appetite for fact. For me there's always been a moral concern, not a philosophical concern, so in that sense I may be in an Anglo-Saxon tradition, which I don't see as bristling with philosophical issues – unlike the Continental novel.

INT: Are you prepared to say what you are working on now?

BU: I'm at a very early phase of a new novel, and all I've got is a sense of a place and a sense of a particular time, and the place is Sicily and the time is the twelfth century during the Norman occupation, which was one of the greatest phases of Sicilian civilisation and life. There were aspects of ethnic and religious collaboration and co-existence which have rarely been reached before or since, and which were crushed. It was a turning point, something that might have been different, a moment on which history hinged. With regard to the plot, I am slowly beginning to get a sense of a story of entrapment, a story of complicated deeds below the surface of power, and agents of that power making arrangements. Which is a bit like the Sicily of today: private arrangements, complicity between political power and organised crime and business interests.

INT: What interests you about the contemporary novel?

BU: Regarding the British novel, I suspect its biggest potential – and we are only talking about a decade or two, because the wider future is imponderable – would lie in dealing with the ethnic and racial complexity of British society, and the way in which adjustments have been made, in a new sort of postcolonial fiction. The prime material for younger writers is the beginning of what I think is a vast potential for fiction, the amalgamations and reservations and adjustments that are being made all the time between generations and between races in an urban society which is at a critical phase. This must or should be the concern. It won't be my concern, but it will be the concern of younger writers.

INT: Finally, what advice would you give to a young writer?

BU: I would say try to disregard all concepts of what kind of novel you feel you should write, or what kind of novel would catch the public taste or might succeed or might be relevant or might be in any way regarded as a winner. Try to look at yourself, try to commune with yourself, and try to determine what sort of a person you are and what kind of a book you're best able to write, and try to do that before you do anything else. So much time is lost by young writers who set out on books they're not equipped to write simply because they think this is the right kind of book for its time, that this is important somehow. These things are insignificant compared to finding a voice for yourself that corresponds to your abilities and the kind of writer you are.

You might be given talent but you're not given a definite sense of what you can do best and the kind of person you are; it's something you have to decide about. After that, you can start thinking about technique – but that comes a long way after!

Select criticism

Boccardi, Mariadale. 'Biography, the Postmodern Last Frontier: Banville, Barnes, Byatt, and Unsworth', *Arts, Littératures & Civilisations du Monde Anglophone* 11 (Oct. 2001), pp. 149–57.

Hulme, Peter. 'The Atlantic World of Sacred Hunger', *New Left Review* 204 (Mar./Apr. 1994), pp. 138–44.

Humphrey, Matthew. 'Foul Play: The Underbelly of Barry Unsworth', *San Francisco Review of Books* 21: 1 (Jan.–Feb. 1996), pp. 18–20.

Kemp, Peter. 'Barry Unsworth', in Jay Parini, ed., *British Writers*: *Supplement VII*. New York: Scribner's, 2002.

Sarvan, Charles. 'Paradigms of the Slave Trade in Two British Novels', *Italia Francescana* 23: 1–2 (1996), pp. 1–6.

Trimm, Ryan S. 'The Logical Errors of Matthew Paris: Or, the Violence of Order in Sacred Hunger', in Steven Kaplan, ed., *The Image of Violence in Literature, the Media, and Society* (Pueblo, CO: Society for the Interdisciplinary Study of Social Imagery, University of Southern Colorado, 1992).

Velcic, Vlatka. 'Postmodern and Postcolonial Portrayals of Colonial History: Contemporary Novels about the Eighteenth Century', *Tennessee Philological Bulletin: Proceedings of the Annual Meeting of the Tennessee Philological Association* 38 (2001), pp. 41–8.

9 Fay Weldon

Pat Wheeler and Jenny Newman

Fay Weldon, prolific and above all else professional, has published over twenty novels, and also short stories, essays, children's books, and radio and television plays (including early episodes of the serial *Upstairs Downstairs*). She began as an advertising copywriter, a profession she used to develop her famously honed prose, with its stylish layout and words spaced and placed for maximum effect. Her career as a novelist took off with the now iconic *Down Among the Women*, a darkly comic look at the female members of three highly distinctive generations. Through a succession of witty, suggestive novels – including *Praxis*, *Puffball* and *The Cloning of Joanna May* – Weldon continued to ask hard questions about the nature of 'femininity', while satirising women's masochism and their readiness to comply with what society expects. Her plots, however, always have moments of choice, where her characters may – if they dare – challenge convention and learn to think for themselves.

Her audience widened when *The Life and Loves of a She-Devil* was adapted for British television and then made into a Hollywood film starring Roseanne Barr and Meryl Streep. A subsequent novel, *Big Women*, began as a Channel 4 serial about the rise and fall of a feminist publishing house, and Weldon has also adapted several classic novels for television. With her wayward sex appeal and financial insecurity, the typical Weldon character can be seen to take after the many eighteenth- and nineteenth-century heroines who learn the limitations of romance and the value of financial independence.

Weldon has recently written a memoir, *Auto da Fay*, which charts her early life in England and New Zealand, and her upbringing in a strong, matriarchal family of writers. Though her fiction usually ends on an optimistic note, in Weldon's view twentieth-century feminist hopes have not been fully realised, and she still sees women as disadvantaged, though in unanticipated ways.

Weldon has been the recipient of a number of awards, including the Writers Guild Award, 1973, the Giles Cooper Award, 1978 and the Los Angeles Times Award, 1989. In 1979 *Praxis* was shortlisted for the Booker Prize and in 1996 Weldon received the PEN/Macmillan Silver Pen Award for *Wicked Women*. She was appointed a CBE in 2001.

Key works

■ Novels

The Fat Woman's Joke. London: MacGibbon & Kee, 1967.

Down Among the Women. London: Heinemann, 1971.

Words of Advice. London: Samuel French, 1974.

Female Friends. London: Heinemann, 1975.

Remember Me. London: Hodder & Stoughton, 1976.

Little Sisters. London: Hodder & Stoughton, 1978.

Praxis. London: Hodder & Stoughton, 1978.

Puffball. London: Hodder & Stoughton, 1980.

The President's Child. London: Hodder & Stoughton, 1982.

The Life and Loves of a She-Devil. London: Hodder & Stoughton, 1983.

The Shrapnel Academy. London: Hodder & Stoughton, 1986.

The Heart of the Country. London: Hutchinson, 1987.

The Hearts and Lives of Men. London: Heinemann, 1987.

The Rules of Life. London: Hutchinson, 1987.

Leader of the Band. London: Hodder & Stoughton, 1988.

The Cloning of Joanna May. London: Collins, 1989.

Darcy's Utopia. London: Collins, 1990.

Growing Rich. London: HarperCollins, 1992.

Life Force. London: HarperCollins, 1992.

Affliction. London: HarperCollins, 1993.

Angel, All Innocence. London: Bloomsbury, 1995.

Splitting. London: Flamingo, 1995.

Wicked Women. London: Flamingo, 1995.

Worst Fears. London: Flamingo, 1996.

Big Women. London: Flamingo, 1997.

Rhode Island Blues. London: Flamingo, 2000.

The Bulgari Connection. London: Flamingo, 2001.

Mantrapped. London: HarperCollins, 2004 (forthcoming).

■ Autobiography

Auto da Fay. London: Flamingo, 2002.

■ Short stories

Watching Me, Watching You. London: Hodder & Stoughton, 1981.

Polaris and Other Stories. London: Hodder & Stoughton, 1985.

Moon Over Minneapolis. London: HarperCollins, 1991.

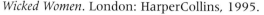
Wicked Women. London: HarperCollins, 1995.
A Hard Time to be a Father. London: Flamingo, 1998.
Nothing to Wear and Nowhere to Hide. London: Flamingo, 2002.

■ Other writing

Letters to Alice: On First Reading Jane Austen. London: Michael Joseph, 1984.
Rebecca West. London: Penguin, 1985.
'Towards a Humorous View of the Universe', *Women's Studies: An
    Interdisciplinary Journal*, 15: 1.3 (1988), pp. 309–11.
Sacred Cows. London: Chatto & Windus, 1989.
Corinthians: The Canon Pocket Bible Series. Edinburgh: Canongate, 1998.
The Lady Is a Tramp: Portraits of Catherine Bailey (with David Bailey). London:
    Thames & Hudson, 1995.
Godless in Eden. London: Flamingo, 1999.

INT: You have written short stories, plays for stage and radio, a libretto,
        children's fiction, an autobiography and over twenty novels, as well as
        many polemical pieces. What do you see as the roots of your
        inspiration?

FW: Indignation is the root of my inspiration. You have to want to write,
        and you have to have something to say, otherwise there's not much
        point. I come from a family of writers, so it didn't seem like anything
        extraordinary.

        I began by working in advertising, where I wrote television
        commercials: little stories aimed at selling a product. Advertising gives
        you a sense of an audience, and I learnt through close association with
        typographers about the mechanics of reading: the importance of short
        paragraphs, and of space on the page. Then it occurred to me that a
        play was just a longer story selling an idea, so I wrote a radio play
        called *The Fat Woman's Joke*, and then plays for television; until I began
        to feel the restrictions of the form: some of the lines would be cut or
        the actor would be wearing the wrong expression, or the set designer
        would make everything look much nicer than I thought it ought to.

        I turned *The Fat Woman's Joke* into a novel – a form over which, of
        course, I had total control. Next I wrote *Down Among the Women*,
        because I couldn't find the book I wanted to read about the dire
        predicament of women, and the bizarre way in which they were both
        treated and regarded; and then I went on to short stories and stage
        plays. All these forms are very different, so it takes some time to

discover the rules; but once you have learnt them you can click into any one of them, almost as if it was a computer. The ability to write in different forms has a lot to do with timing.

INT: You have said that reading has always been your passion. What did you read as you were growing up?

FW: I started very young, and liked fantasy more than reality – Enid Blyton didn't appeal. I began with Hans Christian Andersen, the Brothers Grimm and the Andrew Lang fairy books. Then I went on to authors like E. Nesbit and Rider Haggard. When I'd read all the books in the Christchurch children's library I was allowed to join the adult one, under supervision. When you look at those books now you can see how complex they are; and yet as a child you could get to the essence of them, understanding instinctively what you probably didn't know rationally. You also had to work at uncovering story and plot, which meant that you learnt to skip, which the younger generation doesn't know how to do. Skipping is an active form of reading, because you are controlling what's going on, if only by judging the writer. The books I read as a child were written before the age of film, so it was customary to have long descriptions. I developed the art of getting to the nugget of the story, which is useful today when judging competitions. I never felt it was wrong to skip, whereas many people now think that you should read a book from cover to cover. You might almost say that books nowadays are so plainly and carefully written that you don't need to learn to skip.

Later I read and responded to the prefaces of George Bernard Shaw, and to H. G. Wells, Sinclair Lewis, and all those socially minded, save-the-world writers. I think that as a novelist you are a reporter of your times as well as a writer of stories.

INT: You were in analysis as a young woman, before you became known as a writer. Did that process enable you to create bolder and more truthful narratives?

FW: My views on psychoanalysis have changed over the years, and now I believe that people's interior thoughts are probably better left chaotic. My resistance springs from the fact that psychoanalysis may be a limitation: it doesn't allow you to expand your comprehension of yourself, and may even alter it in some way. Nor does psychoanalysis necessarily enable you to tell a more truthful narrative. On the other hand, it helps you to finish your sentences! As you listen to what is going on in your head, you learn to distinguish between a thought and a feeling, and to understand what a train of thought is, which is useful when it comes to putting things down on paper. I don't know if psychoanalysis did anything for my moral, mental or psychic health, but it did help me to write. Any fictional character's ability to move out of the present probably depends on their understanding of what went before: which becomes a plot point, or back story.

INT: Your eponymous heroine Praxis is like a modern-day Oedipus, who unlike the classical Oedipus manages to learn from her past.

FW: *Praxis* was a fictionalised essay on feminism. I listed all the pejorative terms that men use against women, such as 'adulteress', 'murderess', 'whore'. My aim was to explain why women sometimes have to become these things, if only temporarily, in order to achieve anything. Praxis commits all the big crimes – for instance, she sleeps with her father quite knowingly – but you're not meant to lose sympathy with her, much, because she finds herself in a series of situations from which there's no other way out. Likewise in *The Life and Loves of a She-Devil*: the first thing Ruth does after leaving her husband, Bobbo, is to have sex with Carver, the whiskery, wrinkled old caretaker. Rules sometimes have to be broken if we are to become free. The only power that women had over men was their power to select a mate. If you could lose that basic sexual discrimination that women have and are meant to have, if you could break that physical taboo, then breaking mental taboos became easier. You could begin to see things for real.

INT: You have examined women's issues from the early seventies, when you wrote the iconic *Down Among the Women*, through novels such as *The Cloning of Joanna May*, to the more recent *Big Women*, in which you describe the rise and fall of a women's publishing house. How far do you think your fiction charts the changes in feminism?

FW: Feminism hasn't changed, and that's its problem. The world changes, but the feminist view of it tends to stay rooted in the past – as does that of any political movement. Feminism is now almost as outmoded as Marxism, simply because it no longer applies. That doesn't mean it didn't apply at the time, because of course it did; nor does it mean that all those arguments and battles were in vain. Feminists achieved what they set out to achieve, and then the battlefield shifted. The predicament of women is probably just as bad as ever it was, but the problems are now elsewhere. Feminists can't move on, or attend to those things, while they go on seeing women as victims.

My view is that women's physiology holds them back, and not much else – if 'holds them back' means not letting them be on an equal basis with men. The gap in pay had to do with the fact that women had children, and allowing for that they've done incredibly well. Childbearing is a major factor in anyone's working life, affecting her capacity to earn, and to focus on the things that the patriarchy wanted men – who were also wage slaves – to focus on. If you have a baby you can't go off to work and run the company – though only one in a hundred men ever ran the company anyway.

Today's young women are wonderfully powerful – like the young Byzantia in *Down Among the Women* – until they decide to have babies. Many of them decide not to, and I think that is a misfortune, because you end up living like a man – and why not, really? Other women would rather not have a man involved with the rearing of their child, because then they have to argue with them all the time. I don't see that the sum of happiness is much improved, because the problem of earning money and having a child is exactly what it used to be, only worse, because these days you may have to wait before having a family. Not to have children because you can't afford it, or because society's against you, or because you have to go out to work, or can't fit it into your diary, is a blow against women's rights. This pressure is not put upon women by feminists, but by capitalism under the cloak of feminism, turning everybody into wage slaves and consumers, including children.

INT: At the end of *The Life and Loves of a She-Devil* Ruth says, 'Somehow it is not a matter of male or female, after all; it never was, merely of power.' Do you feel that this notion still fuels your fiction?

FW: Everything seems to me to be about power. If the financial power moves from one member of the household to the other, the conversation changes. The one without power says, 'Why do you leave your dirty knickers for me to pick up?' and the one with the power says, 'Why do you cook the same food every night?' It's not about gender: it's about the disgruntlement of living a life you'd rather not live.

Men were always on the sidelines in my fiction; they're just more on the sidelines now, because women's economic and biological need for them isn't as great as it was. Men have become a sort of optional extra, like air conditioning in the car – nice to have, but you can manage without it. I think my views echo the changes in the outside world; but one changes oneself as one grows older, so there are two variables. You see things differently and there is a different world to see.

INT: You once said, 'I have to examine a proposition in literary terms without necessarily knowing the answers.' Is that still part of your working method?

FW: At the start of a novel you cannot always foresee the last paragraph, but the way you set things up suggests how they're going to end; or else you discover what's going to happen about a third of the way through. Then you can write the final paragraph, and get from here to there, having a good time on the way. A lot of the fiction-writing process is not thought out, but inspirational. All you can do at the start is set yourself problems, and give your characters a background which isn't going to tie up.

Take the opening sentence of *Rhode Island Blues:* ' "I'm old enough to speak the truth," said my grandmother, her voice bouncing over the Atlantic waves, ridiculously girlish.' It was inspired by something my own mother had said to me. She was worrying because she felt she'd been tactless, and I told her that she was old enough to speak the truth. My mother then said, 'Well, they can always put it down to dementia!' *Rhode Island Blues* is about age, and wisdom, and the difficult gap between Felicity's view of herself and the world, and the view of Sophia, her granddaughter. It's also about the similarity between these two generations when you leave out the middle one by rendering it insane, so it only exists as a plot point.

Rhode Island Blues is also about the unwisdom of digging up the past. I wrote it with a sense of discovery, because for some of the time I did not know what was going to happen next, or whether William Johnson was going to turn out good or bad. For all I knew at the start, Nurse Dawn was absolutely wise! The thesis proved to be that the old can gamble and the young can't, because the young know too much. There were all sorts of interesting points to be made on the way; but the novel as a whole doesn't have the quality of parable which I like fiction to have, or as much of a subtext.

INT: But *Rhode Island Blues* prompts us to think about losing – and retaining – memory; which is paralleled in the younger woman's quest for her family.

FW: Perhaps you can't help having a subtext, because your readers will always detect one for you! But as a writer, you do have to trust your unconscious. You can be analytical later, but not at the time of writing. That remains a sort of sleepwalk.

INT: Have you evolved a preferred narrative strategy?

FW: The strategy evolves in order to fit what you mean to do. Some things are obvious; for example, you can write a short novel in the first person if it involves young women, because they seem to interest the world at large. Their consciousness is a puzzle that you just have to follow through to the end of the book. But in general the trouble with first-person narrative is that you as author are not allowed to know any more than your narrator.

I avoided that problem in *The President's Child* by making the character Maya work as an author surrogate. Though she speaks in the first person, her name and her blindness are meant to suggest that she has great wisdom and knows everything – which is not necessarily true of blind people, but a frequent assumption. Then there are my 'Dear Reader' books, which are fun because you seldom have to rewrite them. You do the most rewriting when you are using an authorial voice, because you have to keep that voice consistent from beginning to end, which could mean for a period of six months.

INT: In a single novel, such as *The Hearts and Lives of Men*, or *The President's Child*, or *The Cloning of Joanna May*, you often include strands from different genres – science fiction, romance, *Bildungsroman*, thriller – and different narrative voices. Why do you so often adopt this strategy?

FW: You have to keep your readers turning the page, and you have to keep yourself writing. When you need a break you can move from one voice to another, or else from one mode to another, or you can feed in a kind of think voice. You can do anything in a novel, if you can get away with it, which means being convinced enough, and keeping things consistent and in some kind of internal pattern. *The Life and Loves of a She-Devil*, for example, goes in threes. It begins with Ruth's voice, which is a complaint or a dirge. Next you see her through the author's eyes, and then through the eyes of another character. The technique reflects life and its different rhythms. Your view of the world shifts several times between when you wake up and when you go to bed.

INT: Your fiction often draws on specialised areas, such as cloning, or modern weaponry, or plastic surgery. What part does research play in your writing?

FW: My general theory is that if you need to research a particular topic, then you'd better not write the novel in question, because that's not what you're there for. If you have a guess, on the other hand, your guess is usually correct. For *The Cloning of Joanna May*, for instance, I knew about cloning anyway, although I had to invent a method of doing it back in the 1950s. Today's science fantasy often becomes tomorrow's science fact, because if you can so much as think of it some scientist can and will do it, eventually. I made my scientists use electric shock, and I actually got it right: that was what was later done with Dolly the sheep. But everyone thought that what I'd written on the subject in *The Cloning of Joanna May* was science fiction, and that the rest of the novel was true, which I'd made up. So I thought that I might as well make up everything, and it will either be believed or not believed.

Sometimes you read a non-fiction book that's so interesting that you want to bring the issues to life in a novel. *The Shrapnel Academy*, for example, was born out of a book on the history and development of weapons, which described the extraordinary business of how a defensive weapon turns into an offensive weapon, and how the situation then escalates.

INT: In *Letters to Alice* you wrote that the 'writers who get the best response from readers are those who offer a happy ending through some kind of moral development'. Do you still wish to change the way in which your readers respond to the world?

FW: I still feel that many people are given to self-deception, and I'd like them to consider things rather more than they do. For me, it's part of a desire to teach: I try to present what is happening to readers who don't see it for themselves. This started with my early feminist novels, because it baffled me that people couldn't see what was going on. I still don't think that women see the degree of their exploitation, and how helpless they are, which is, if you like, new ground for fiction.

I think that my readers believe I'm one of them, just as I think they're one of me. It's a mutual thing; but if you like I have the gift of the gab and can put things down on the page for them, and say, 'Well, how's that, then?' I can do something they can't, which is dramatise an idea, or focus it; but I feel I am writing for my readers, rather than remaining apart from them. I'm just the chairman at the top of the table – or it's probably a round table now! I'm the facilitator and have been put in charge, and am, I hope, representing my readers' best part, not their worst, as I hope governments represent the best will of the people and not the worst.

INT: In *The Rules of Life* you suggest that fiction may be the new religion. Do your characters sometimes personify good and evil – like, for example, the chauffeur in *Growing Rich*?

FW: Bad characters are usually more interesting than good ones, and easier to write and to read about, because we only have to let certain parts of ourselves off the leash. The chauffeur in *Growing Rich* represents self-interest, and tells you what you want to do instead of what you ought to do. This message is especially important for women, who are prone to do the latter. But beyond his glittery eyes he doesn't have any supernatural powers.

I see evil as being on a lesser scale than God; it's something real and almost tangible which happens and attacks and goes away again. I wouldn't wish to personify God, because I don't think it's my place; although *The Bulgari Connection* does have my first saint in it. I was paid to write the novel by Bulgari, the jewellers, for a limited edition of 750 copies to be given away at a grand dinner. It's a sort of product placement novel, and because I made no attempt to do anything other than fulfil a brief, I managed to write something very interesting. Now it's been brought out by my usual publishers, so the novel has ended up looking respectable.

INT: How do you see your development over your career as a writer?

FW: I suppose it's a development, because the more you write the easier it becomes. Or rather, seeing how you can best say something becomes easier, and therefore what you say can become more complex, because you now find it possible to say it. You're as complex as your technical skill will allow you to be, and as that skill gets greater you can take on more. But again, it's not conscious. Only on looking back do I see that my novels tend to fall into groups of three. There might be three divorce novels, or three 'Dear Reader' novels, or three 'I hate therapy' novels, like *Affliction*, *Worst Fears* and *Splitting*, of which *Splitting* is the most interesting. The divorce novels are linked by theme rather than by style, whereas my 'Dear Reader' novels are linked by style rather than content. You give your readers recipes, and vary them from one novel to the next – rather like a painter, who will move from one style to another; but not quite so obvious.

Sometimes the novels come about accidentally. *Big Women*, for instance, started out as a television series, and I turned it into a novel because I'd done half the work. Then I published a lot of short stories, some of which had been written quite a long time ago and forgotten. You find your writing level without setting out to.

INT: Do you think that writing can be taught?

FW: Only if people have something they want to say. When you say to some would-be writers, 'Well, what do you want to write?' they have no idea. They just want to be 'writers'. I never wanted to be a writer, and I think the desire is a counter-indication. A better way of identifying promise is to look at the number of books that somebody's read – people often say they want to be writers when they haven't read anything at all. As a writer you want to write the same sort of fiction that you want to read. When you've read a lot of novels and found that no one else is writing that particular kind of book, you write it yourself, and find your own way through it. Teaching people to write can do no harm at all; but unless they have a need I don't think they will learn.

Sometimes you have a lot of sympathy for beginner writers, and can tell that someone is probably too young, or doesn't know how to begin, but actually does have something to say. Then you can show them short cuts, or explain that there's more than one way of skinning a cat. You can also help them to see that they're not doomed, they're free! In other words, they don't have to pay too much reverence to what they have already written, just because it's theirs. People have an amazing respect for something they've put on a page, as if they're not allowed to change it! But in general I feel that not much about writing is teachable or learnable, which is hard cheese on all those creative writing courses. Writing is something you know about innately.

That is not to say that I haven't taught my share of Arvon courses; but there are so many of them now that I no longer enjoy doing them. The classes are full of people on arts administration modules, who want to know how it's done, rather than of people who actually write. The students have often been taught by tutors who aren't writers, according to some theory of what writing is – which tends to restrict, as I said in *Letters to Alice* (which is now being taught, I notice). Standards of writing are much higher now than they were, and many people are technically able to write very well, and express what they think very well. When it comes to the relevant kind of invention, however, they often fail; but invention is a rare thing anyway. Although their writing is seldom inelegant or bad or crude, they don't seem to say very much because they don't have very much to say. They have style and no substance. It may be a matter of teaching creative writing to too many people.

Writing has to be worth reading! If you consider the number of person hours involved in writing a novel, for example, you realise that you have to say something worth saying, something which informs or enlightens. Of course, fiction can just entertain; but if it sets out to do anything more it has to succeed, or you bore people to bits. You have to have something to say that people want to read, and you have to believe that your perception of people or events is helpful or interesting. And some effort has to go into it.

INT: You have always been quick to embrace new things, such as television and film. Now you are writing on the World Wide Web.

FW: I was writing a serial, so I didn't have too much to do at any one time; but after about seven episodes I didn't want to do any more. If one person had said, 'Why have you stopped writing?' I would have continued! There is absolutely no response, you see, and that's when you discover that you need a publisher. You discover you need book form. You discover you need an editor, and people with all those other skills which feed into what you write in order to produce something that people want to read. For me, who has always thought, 'Well, it's only the content that matters. Who cares about all this?', it has been something of a lesson.

INT: In what directions will your future writing be going?

FW: I recently wrote a radio short story about Boadicea which Vanessa Redgrave read brilliantly. Now she wants me to write an hour-long monologue for the stage. I've also been commissioned to write a radio play, and somebody wants to turn *The Life and Loves of a She-Devil* into an opera. But the main thing is my next novel, and so far I don't know what that will be. If somebody offered me another product placement novel, which I could do without thinking, I might discover that I had done something very interesting again, because the process takes irrationality to an extreme.

INT: You are a well-known commentator on the literary scene. Who do you see as the most promising British novelists?

FW: I very much like Liz Jensen's fiction. Her latest novel, *War Crimes for the Home*, was a big step forward from her earlier ones, which were domestic fantasies. Now she seems to be turning towards political or social fantasy. And I enjoy the fiction of Helen Fielding, and Sally Emerson's quirky novel, *Broken Bodies*, which is partly set in the British Museum. I also like Helen Simpson, who wrote *Hey, Yeh, Right, Get a Life*. She's a proper writer, who uses language in a way that you wish more people could.

At some stage a novelist needs to take on society, which is difficult to do, and explains why you often can't think of any outstanding younger writers. Zadie Smith is good, and clever too. She's a bit young to do what she does, but she's taking something on in a way which very few will or can, I think because society is changing so fast, and political correctness sometimes makes writing difficult. There are all sorts of things that you can't say nowadays. Again. If you write what you really think, your friends won't speak to you, or else some organisation comes after you. I'm already in trouble with Islam, and registered as an Islamophobe, because I once said that I didn't think the Koran was a good poem to base a society on! As a statement, this seems to me very mild. I could probably say the same about any religious poem, including the Bible.

What makes writers is the habit of outsiderism. If that is forbidden, either by self-censorship or outside censorship, the novelist is left with a problem, and goes on to write films instead of novels, which are hard enough to write anyway. The young, it seems to me, are no longer allowed to be subversive, but are brainwashed into endorsing certain assumptions, such as: ecology is good. A young writer came up to me recently and said things like, 'I know I have to work hard at this', or 'I know I haven't done enough.' I wanted to say to her, 'Where is your aggro? Where is your belief that you know more than everybody else? Why are you being so well-behaved and good?' And they somehow all are, you see. There's no room for dissent in their over-examined lives, and they all excuse themselves before they begin.

In the sixties, on the other hand, we had something to fight against; today there's so little because the opposition has stepped back and is incorporated into things and agrees with you, so for young people there is nowhere to go, other than into delinquency and drugs. If you get agitated about the condition of the old-age homes, for example, the authorities will just say, 'Yes, we understand, and we'll put more money into them.' It becomes hard to sustain outrage when there's always somebody there before you saying, 'Yes, we know all that.'

INT: Do you see any significant trends in late twentieth-century or early twenty-first-century fiction, or do you think it's eclectic?

FW: There's 'chick lit' and 'lad lit' and all kinds of other new categories, but in a way they're all about marketing, so the truth about what's going on can be difficult to detect. I know that a lot of good novels, which five years ago would have been published, are not being published now, and they're often the more sensitive, intelligent ones, which don't have a particular marketing angle. That includes novels by older writers which don't get published because they're too thoughtful, or too gentle or too slow. The editorial departments will always want to do them and the marketing departments will always say no, and at the moment the marketing departments hold sway. You find that a lot of new fiction stems from women's magazine features which have been turned into what you might call 'issue novels'. Non-fiction, however, is in a healthy state, including biography, and science journalism, which is incredibly good at making what seems impossible to understand really simple.

In the end very good novels do get through and always will, because there will always be somebody out there who is somehow going to recognise them. And publishing changes all the time. The climate gets bad and then there seems to be a swing back to what's better, because we have readers who will always want something good, or interesting, or which absorbs them, or which seems to reflect what actually happened, and not what's going on in the centre of London, or down on the housing estate. That kind of reader never changes, no matter how marketing departments try to make them.

There is always a shortage of good writing, or writing that holds people's attention and takes a new look at things. I think it surfaces in the end. I hope it does.

Select criticism

■ Books

Barreca, Regina, ed., *Fay Weldon's Wicked Fictions*. Lebanon, NH: University Press of New England, 1994.

Dowling, Finoula. *Fay Weldon's Fiction*. Cranbury, NJ: Fairleigh Dickinson University Press, 1999.

Faulks, Lana. *Fay Weldon*. New York: Twayne, 1998.

■ Articles and chapters

Achilles, Jochen. 'Fay Weldon's *Darcy's Utopia* and the Utopian Tradition', in Beate Neumeier, ed., *Engendering Realism and Postmodernism*. Amsterdam: Rodopi, 2001.

Cane, Aleta F. 'Demythifying Motherhood in Three Novels by Fay Weldon', in Andrea O'Reilly Herrera, Elizabeth Mahn Nollen and Sheila Reitzel Foor, eds, *Family Matters in the British and American Novel*. Bowling Green, OH: Popular, 1997.

Ford, Betsy. 'Belladonna Speaks: Fay Weldon's Waste Land Revision in *The Cloning of Joanna May*', *West Virginia University Philological Papers* 38 (1992), pp. 322–33.

Gholson, Craig. 'Fay Weldon', *BOMB* 30 (1990), pp. 45–7.

Hebert, Ann Marie. 'Rewriting the Feminine Script: Fay Weldon's Wicked Laughter', *Critical Matrix: The Princeton Journal of Women, Gender, and Culture* 7: 1 (1993), pp. 21–40.

Knutsen, Karen. 'War Crimes and the Crime Novel: Fay Weldon's *The Shrapnel Academy*', *A Journal of English Language and Literature* 82: 5 (Oct. 2001), pp. 437–49.

Kumar, Mina. 'Interview: Fay Weldon', *Belles Lettres* 10: 2 (1995), pp. 16–18.

Mitchell, Margaret E. 'Fay Weldon', in George Stade and Carol Howard, eds, *British Writers: Supplement IV*. New York: Scribner's, 1997.

Müller, Anja. 'Feminine Misogyny and Sisterly Undercurrents: Cases of Groundless Solidarity in Fay Weldon's *Remember Me*', in Beate Neumeier, ed., *Engendering Realism and Postmodernism*. Amsterdam: Rodopi, 2001.

Newman, Jenny. '"See me as Sisyphus, but having a good time": the fiction of Fay Weldon', in Robert Hosmer, ed., *Contemporary British Women Writers: Texts and Strategies*. London: Macmillan, 1993.

Smith, Patricia Juliana. 'Weldon's *The Life and Loves of a She-Devil*', *Explicator* 51: 4 (1993), pp. 55–7.

Stanley, William. '"Like a Nuclear Blast": Fay Weldon's Explosion of the Military Order', *The Shrapnel Academy, Literature Interpretation Theory* 11: 4 (2001), pp. 351–84.

Stein, Thomas. 'Strategies of Subversion in Fay Weldon's Miss Jacobs Stories', in Beate Neumeier, ed., *Engendering Realism and Postmodernism*. Amsterdam: Rodopi, 2001.

Wilde, Alan. '"Bold, but Not Too Bold": Fay Weldon and the Limits of Poststructuralist Criticism', *Contemporary Literature* 29: 3 (1988), pp. 403–19.

Young, Pauline. 'Selling the Emperor's New Clothes: Fay Weldon as Contemporary Folklorist', *Folklore in Use* 2: 1 (1994), pp. 103–13.

Irvine Welsh

Nahem Yousaf and Pat Wheeler

Irvine Welsh, one of Britain's most original and revelatory writers of novels, short stories and stage plays, first came to prominence in the early 1990s as one of a group of writers on the burgeoning Scottish literary scene. As he says below, his initial aim was to dismiss the 'culturally elitist baggage, which imposed hegemony over other voices'. The 'remaking' of Scottish identities played out in his work was to prove extraordinarily effective. Welsh stakes out his claim on Scottish fiction, and from *Acid House* to *Porno* his work captures the alienation and fragmentation of life as lived within Edinburgh communities devastated by the effects of years of Thatcherite economic policies.

It is Welsh's bestselling novel, *Trainspotting*, published in 1993, that most memorably explores the topography and subculture of inner-city Edinburgh. *Trainspotting* became a sensational success: shortlisted for the Booker Prize, it also has the dubious claim to fame of being one of the most shoplifted books of all time. The novel has been adapted for both the stage and the cinema (director Danny Boyle, 1996). *The Acid House*, which followed, was also adapted for the cinema (director Paul McGuigan, 1998).

Welsh's writing is creative, startling and energising; he deploys a variety of innovative narrative devices and techniques. In *Trainspotting* the narrative is 'authentically' demotic, passed from character to character, from voice to voice, to anatomise a side of a city that was previously unknown in literature. The narrator of *Maribou Stork Nightmares* (1995) is in a coma throughout and *Filth* (1998) is partly narrated by a parasitic worm in the gut of a policeman. *Glue* tells the story of four Edinburgh 'schemies' over thirty years of their lives and *Porno* (2002) revisits the scenes of his earlier work, *Trainspotting*, to look again at Edinburgh through the eyes of some of the characters who have now become part of British popular culture. *Porno* moves from the metropolitan centre of London back to Edinburgh, a reverse journey to a kind of nationhood, one built on a new notion of identity and place. In *Porno* Welsh reflects on a new monster devouring Scotland: global consumerism and capitalism, the pornography of greed that he sees as devouring us all in the end. It has been said that Welsh examines the 'addictions of our baser natures', yet there is a tacit morality that underpins the degeneracy.

Key works

■ Fiction

Trainspotting. London: Secker & Warburg, 1993.

The Acid House. London: Jonathan Cape, 1994.

Marabou Stork Nightmares. London: Jonathan Cape, 1995.

Ecstasy: Three Tales of Chemical Romance. London: Jonathon Cape, 1996.

Filth. London: Jonathan Cape, 1998.

Glue. London: Jonathan Cape, 2001.

Porno. London: Jonathan Cape, 2002.

■ Select drama

4 Play, by Harry Gibson, Keith Wyatt, Irvine Welsh. London: Vintage, 2001.

You'll Have Had Your Hole. London: Methuen, 1998.

■ Select other works

Shang-a-lang: Life as an International Pop Idol, by Les McKeown and Lynne Elliott, with a foreword by Irvine Welsh. Edinburgh: Mainstream, 2003.

Orphans, by Peter Mullan, Irvine Welsh. Suffolk: Screenpress, 1999.

The First Black Footballer: An Absence of Memory, by Phil Vasili, Irvine Welsh. London: Frank Cass, 1998.

Drugs and the Party Line, ed. Kevin Williamson, introd. Irvine Welsh. Edinburgh: Rebel Inc., 1996.

INT: How and when did you begin writing?

IW: My family were readers, but not really bookish. We lived in a small council flat so there wasn't a lot of space to keep books: no shelves, little storage space. So I grew up seeing books not as possessions, but as communal: things that circulated around. To this day when I finish a book, I leave it on the Underground for somebody to pick up. I'm not too sure about the writing; I remember somebody saying sometime, Jim Kelman or Janice Galloway seem to come to mind, that the real question should be 'When did you stop writing?' I don't know about the premise, namely that writing is a human activity which we just do and then sacrifice to the needs of the economy when we become wage slaves, although I suppose that my own experience bears this out.

I wrote compositions at school and stopped when I started work at sixteen as an apprentice television and radio mechanic. I remember meeting Mrs Tait, my English teacher, in the street. She was a very good teacher, a very good person, and very encouraging. Mrs Tait once got us to do a school magazine, which Jim Carnie (the deputy head) confiscated because of its content. There was a lot of sex and violence in it. I remember her arguing with him about it in the corridor. I wanted to speak up, take her side, but I couldn't say anything. I was too inarticulate and servile in the face of his authority. I suppose I was just a kid, and had I intervened I would have only made things worse. But I felt cowardly and weak. Jim Carnie wasn't a bad guy (he was a Hibs fan after all!). He was only doing his job as he saw it and trying to stop his Scheme school descending into anarchy.

I met Mrs Tait in the street and she asked me if I was still writing. The question amused, then shamed, then eventually challenged me. For all the encouragement she gave me I still thought that writing was something you only did in English lessons at school. I coughed out something articulate like 'naw'. She looked earnestly at me, and said 'You should.' That stuck with me. Thank you, Mrs Tait and the few other teachers I met like you. Every schemie needs at least one. Mrs Tait gave us some great reading, which I confess I didn't fully appreciate at the time but I've since tracked back to, such as Lewis Grassic Gibbon's trilogy *A Scots Quair*, George Douglas Brown's *The House with the Green Shutters*, and Hugh McDiarmid's writing.

INT: Who are your main literary influences and how did you find your own voice as a writer?

IW: My main influences were relatives and neighbours; they were brilliant storytellers. I was hungry to hear stories as a kid, and the people around me were more than happy to oblige. I listened to women telling tales of their families, men talking of working life, tales of thieving or choring, other kids at school just rapping about what they got up to, older kids with their fighting and shagging talk. It's that old Celtic oral tradition, by fuck you could talk, but you'd never, ever think of writing it down. Writing was seen as a 'poofy' kind of thing where I came from, so my early attempts at it were a bit like my first attempts at masturbation; bitter, sly and tainted with some notion of sin. Some might say that little has changed! When I came to write properly, for want of a better term, all those voices were still birling around in my head.

I got into reading big time one summer, in the sense of taking responsibility for my own reading rather than waiting for my Auntie Betty's Catherine Cooksons to come to me. I started with Robert Louis Stevenson, then Charles Dickens, then discovered William McIlvanney's *Laidlaw*. That was a breakthrough book for me. It was liberating to experience great writing about a place and a people I could recognise. It set me off into taking an interest in contemporary Scottish literature. There was always a big 'Scottish book' of the time: Kelman's *The Busconductor Hines*, Gray's *Lanark*, Banks's *The Wasp Factory*, Butlin's *The Sound of my Voice*. Kelman was another step from McIlvanney with his use of narrative. I think he's a massively influential figure, and in a positive way, a writer's writer. I got into Russian literature, Dostoevsky and Tolstoy, then US literature, Burroughs, Bukowsky, Wolfe, Updike, F. Scott Fitzgerald, Cormac McCarthy, Faulkner, the lot. I got into everything American. With English literature it was Jane Austen, the Brontës, George Eliot, the sort of stuff that I'd resisted, hated, at school. And Shakespeare . . . fuck, how I grew to love Shakespeare. Once you liberate that stuff from the authoritarian context it is taught in, and can just see it as literature, it really starts to stand up. European . . . don't get me started, I could go on and on. Somebody recommends a book and one thing leads to another. I'll still get and give the odd telephone message: READ THIS NOW. Duncan McLean and Kevin Williamson and myself were into that, phoning each other up saying: THIS IS THE ONE.

Kelman's *The Busconductor Hines* was an important book for the generation of Scottish writers I came out of, which was Edinburgh 1990. Glasgow was trying to reinvent itself with the City of Culture stuff, and you had the 'workers' city' reaction to that, in which Glasgow writers were prominent. In Edinburgh it was more hedonistic but writers were discovering through various means that they were all doing roughly the same thing in isolation; Alan Warner, Paul Reekie, Barry Graham, Kevin Williamson, Duncan McLean, Gordon Legge, Rodney Relax and loads more. Some of us were into raving and clubbing and drugs, others preferred folk, skittles and beer. A few were even into writing and literature! Duncan had Clocktower Press and Kevin started Rebel Inc. Barry is often underestimated in all this but I think he was a really inspirational figure for a lot of people because he was spiky and confrontational and stopped the whole thing getting too cosy. It wasn't really a scene as such; the *New York Times* did a piece on the 'Scottish Beats', which was wide of the mark. It was more a loose federation than a movement. Some people were close pals, others never hit it off socially, but all contributed in different ways. There was an energy and focus there, a lot of it provided by Rebel Inc. I think Kevin was the first to understand that something was definitely happening, and to put it into a social/political context; I confess I never really got it that much at the time. I think a lot of that energy was lost as a load of people moved on. Alan went to Ireland, Barry went to America, I went to Holland, Duncan went to Orkney. This wasn't because we had publishing success with London houses as has been suggested. We were all quite nomadic anyway and the real surprise was that we happened to be in Edinburgh at the same time in the first place. I think when Kevin moved Rebel Inc. to Canongate and started to bring out books the scene died a bit. It was the way to go though, and they brought out some excellent stuff. Rebel Inc. also published John King first and I think John's been very influential in encouraging English writers from working-class backgrounds. This is a digression, but what I'm trying to say is that all these people were a great help and a big influence on me. There's been a suggestion that there was some rivalry with the Glasgow-based writers. Nothing is further from the truth. Jim Kelman, Janice Galloway, Janet Fulton-Cook, Tom Leonard, William McIlvanney and many others have been very generous and encouraging to me.

INT: Do you see yourself as writing against the idea of the English novel standing for the British novel?

IW: The Scottish novel is strange, because clearly some form of democracy is at work here. You could put a group of Scottish novelists in a bar and they'd be, socially speaking, a pretty fair representation of Scottish people. If you did the same with the English equivalents, they'd be a pretty fair representation of Oxbridge. I don't think you write against anything; writing should be about affirming your own culture rather than slagging off anybody else's. The problem is that literature in Britain is tied to a culturally elitist baggage, which imposes hegemony over other voices. So by affirming your own culture, you come into opposition with it at some level, whether you aim to or not.

INT: You have captured a Scottish, and specifically Edinburgh, dialect, haven't you?

IW: Nobody had really attempted to catch the Edinburgh dialect of the inner city and Schemes before, at least not to my knowledge. There was a lazy cultural complacency that Edinburgh was Morningside and Miss Jean Brodie and Glasgow was working-class and proletarian. This model is of very limited application if you come from Hyndland or Bearsden or Kelvinside or Hillhead or Niddrie or Muirhouse or Wester Hailes or Gracemount. In fact, most of Glasgow and Edinburgh. Edinburgh dialect makes use of terms like 'chavy' and 'chorin', which originate from the gypsy community, as well as old Lalands Scots and a kind of developing street slang. I liked it because it was more musical and performative to me, more real and honest. The Queen's English is fine for reports but for fiction it's stultifyingly boring. If people tried to talk on the screen or even the stage the way they do in most books they'd be laughed at. Even toffs feel the need to adopt pseudo working-class accents on telly now. Apart from newsreaders, they don't talk like Noel Coward on British television any more.

INT: When you embark on a writing project do you think of potential audiences? For example, do you think about American readers and their struggle with the language you use, or about female readers and their potential reactions to your representations of women?

IW: No. I don't think about that until it's finished. Art creates the product, then after that it's all commerce. The marketing side of things is drab enough to contemplate once you've finished a book without thinking about it while you're writing. Then I can worry myself sick that nobody outside of Leith will be able to read it. Obviously I know I could sell more books in the US, Canada, Australia, New Zealand or South Africa if I compromised a bit on the lingo, but I'm impressed by the people from those countries who are into the books as they stand. They're prepared to make the effort rather than just mindlessly buy what's on the *New York Times* bestseller lists and I think they gain as a result. I'd say that the punters who read my books are far more clued-up and culturally aware than most critics. I get a lot of women readers and they seem to 'get it' better than men. Beyond the superficiality of things, I think I'm a very feminine writer.

INT: A femine writer? How do you feel about the labels that have been attached to your work?

IW: You're always going to be called something. Labels always obscure more than they illuminate though. I've been called loads of things now; if you stick all the labels I've had together, the result might fit me quite well.

INT: You have female characters in lead roles, for example, Samantha, Lorraine, Rebecca, in the short stories. However, they still seem to need male catalysts to act, in order to come to life as it were, don't they?

IW: I've been interested in the madness and marvellousness of male working-class culture but I'm becoming more into women characters as I get older. Part of me thinks that there are some women writers who do women characters so well that it's better to leave them to it. I've got a lot of longstanding female friends. I'd never try it on with them either, it would be like shagging your sister. They often express their astonishment that I don't have more women characters. But my writing is quite masculine in a feminist sort of way!

INT: There are many references to popular culture and music throughout your novels. Does music influence your writing?

IW: Music sets the moods. When I devise a character I think of where they come from, what their sexual predilections are, what records they listen to and 'where they stay, who they lay, what they play' roughly. I've got a lot of albums which are crap, but they are what my characters listen to. It was hard listening to that metal and easy listening MOR stuff for Bruce Robertson in *Filth*. It drove me crazy. Music is a great way of finding character and it works particularly well. I stick on Prince or Barry White or Roger Sanchez and I become Sick Boy. I put on Iggy, Primals, the Fall, the Clash, PIL or the Pistols and I'm Renton. For Begbie I stick on Slade or Oasis. For Spud, it's Frank Zappa or the Alabama 3.

INT: You also mix social realism, surrealism, fantasy and, to an extent, magical realism, don't you?

IW: I think people now are clued-up enough to realise that the novel is written in imaginative space. I like unreliable narrators. I don't think that a lot of the old dichotomies between realism and fantasy exist in narrative any more. People consume culture now through ads, soundbites, video games, music and they're often off their tits on drugs. So the border between realism and fantasy has broken down: if you fantasise, it's real. The reader and the writer operate in their imagination. I think a lot of the ideas around soundbite culture and low attention span come about because more people operate in imaginative space now. It's an essential psychic defence against the encroachment of the world telling us what to buy and who to be.

INT: Do you feel most comfortable writing first-person narration or is the omniscient narrator your favoured vehicle?

IW: It's the straightforward dilemma that every writer faces, how do you do the narrative? Ideologically, I prefer to create the characters and let them narrate, let them lead me. Sometimes you have to compromise and use the godlike authorial voice if you've got loads going on. It's never your conscious choice, it just happens the way it does, sometimes for better, sometimes for worse. It should be driven by character and story though. I try not to dwell on process too much.

INT: Hanif Kureishi wrote and directed *London Kills Me* (1991) which tells the story of drug dealing and using, among other things. When asked about that film's critical reception he spoke about *Trainspotting* as better capturing the mood and time of that particular 'scene'. Do you agree with him that *Trainspotting* came along at the right time to capture a mood?

IW: That's generous of him to say so. I do think it came along at the right time. We've always had rich kids with trust funds and clinics doing loads of drugs until it's time to clean up and get the career online. In the eighties though, drugging up had become a more democratic thing and everyone was at it. Literature hadn't picked up on this; perhaps because a lot of the writers were rich kids with trust funds. *Trainspotting* worked because everybody in it was from and of the same place, and it was a place that hadn't been done to death in popular cultural representations.

INT: How important was it, then, to set *Trainspotting* in the housing projects of Edinburgh?

IW: *Trainspotting* was set in Leith, which is more inner city than housing scheme. But in the eighties the city was awash with AIDS and heroin, and produced a football mob which tore up Scotland. The point is that there was a lot of anger and despair and violence and the view of the place was still 'festival city with genteel Morningside and a few New Town lawyers thrown in!' The problem with that social model is that it doesn't include 90% of the city. I'm not saying *Trainspotting* shows a world that is more inclusive or universal, it doesn't. That's the whole point; let's have as many different truths as we can so that a balanced picture emerges.

INT: That's interesting because in *Trainspotting* Johnny says 'we are all acquaintances now', which Mark (Rents) sees as a 'brilliant metaphor for our times'.

IW: The comment is about the atomisation of our society and the increasing alienation of the individual. We've spawned a monster in global consumer capitalism, which is devouring us, but I think it has to be the way to go.

INT: In the dedication that prefaces *Marabou Stork Nightmares* you thank your family for not being the one in the novel and this has resonance in the way we see Roy as a product of his family and his environment. Is this something you feel strongly about – that we are shaped by forces outside our control?

IW: Yes. The big problem with bad bastards is that some of them are quite nice. They seldom come with the flashing neon sign above their head that says CUNT. We are shaped by all sorts of things, but unlike puppets we've got the opportunity to look up and snip the strings, even if some of them seem like they're made of steel cable at times.

INT: What about the visual impact of the fragmented and stylised narrative in *Marabou Stork Nightmares*. Is it a device to reflect Roy's inner self and his journey to some form of self-knowledge?

IW: I wanted to look at different states of consciousness. Questing is very important for young and not so young men. It's why we join gangs, hang around with people who'll do us no good and whom we sometimes might not even like. I wanted to show how imagination, though proscribed by circumstance, can never be mastered. I like the idea of people living different lives such as in fantasy or dream.

INT: John Strang in *Marabou Stork Nightmares* says that Margaret Thatcher 'is the best fuckin leader Britain's had'. Duncan Ewart in *Glue* and, to a certain extent, Bruce in *Filth*, espouse socialist views. Can you unpack your approach to politics?

IW: I'm not really interested in overt party politics; it's a sideshow, which detracts from the real political issues of the day. I'm interested in the way people come about their beliefs, even if I don't vibe on them personally, in fact especially if I don't. I know what I think therefore I'm not so interested in that. I want to know what others think. I don't think a socialist state could exist in the UK or any other nation state in isolation in the future. When you consider the impact Scotland's had on the modern world with the Scottish enlightenment, and now with the development of globalisation, it's impossible that such a small country, or indeed any country with the possible exception of the USA, could ever have that influence again. In culture, economics and sport, it's all boring economies of scale. Scotland will be like Surrey in ten years' time, which will bear a striking resemblance to New Jersey. Sad, but true. It's after this tiresome phase that things might get interesting. Once we're totally globalised, what does capitalism do for an encore? The answer has to be socialism of some form, either that or blow up the world.

INT: In *Filth* you have a worm narrating events. Is the worm another element in Bruce Robertson's consciousness, and do you see the police as a thoroughly corrupt and corrupting force as well as upholders of state-sanctioned ideology?

IW: I see the worm as Bruce's conscience. I like the idea of parasites, but I'm far more interested in the host. I've never had the big beef with the polis that people imagine from reading *Filth*. I've been locked up loads of times and always deserved it because I've acted like a cunt. We get the police force we as a society deserve. Cops are doing an impossible job now; our daft laws have criminalised most of the population. I think that's why gangster movies and culture are so big now, just about everyone can identify with it to an extent. No, Bruce started out as an environmental health officer. I had some fun with his personal hygiene in the restaurants he was inspecting but when I made him a cop it gave me a chance to go into the power and corruption side of it. Police corruption and accountability and canteen culture are an issue, just look at the newspapers. A week seldom goes by without some sex or race case in one force or another. But the point is that this happens in just about every workplace in the country; in most cases the police are more liberal than the legislators.

INT: You have stated that 'when there is an absence of love, the void is filled by bitterness, anger and resentment'. There doesn't seem to be much love in your books?

IW: I would disagree. I think there's a lot of love in them. Often it's only present by its absence and it's frustrated. I'm primarily a dramatic writer though, and drama is about conflict so I like it to kick a little. I think the overt, calculated absence of love in a book is a massive challenge. Take 'The Undefeated'. It's a modern love story. It's about aspiring to love in a society that is happy to make do with fucking and shopping.

INT: There isn't much love in the collection of stories in *Ecstasy* though, but there is existential despair. These are dark stories with moral ambiguities, yet they are also political in that they address the emptiness at the heart of society.

IW: I don't like *Ecstasy* as much as my other books but some bits in it work quite well. There is more existential angst in it than I generally care for but it seems to me that there is a great big hole in the moral heart of western society. They've filled it in with a shopping mall. I've always regarded *Ecstasy* as a bit of a failed experiment. I don't think I've ever tried to glorify drugs, I don't think you *can* successfully glorify them. People would just laugh if you wrote a book doing that. They'd laugh for a few pages and then go, 'Fuck off . . . ' and throw it down, in exactly the same way they do when the authorities write a leaflet or run an ad condemning drugs. You have to show *why* people do them and what the consequences of that *are*, for themselves and for others. It's as simple and honest as that.

INT: Do you think *Glue* re-established you after the rather negative critical reception to *Filth*?

IW: You're never 'established' by critics, that's the reader's job. *Filth* was my biggest seller outside *Trainspotting* in the UK. I wasn't aware it was judged negatively, but I'm the sort of writer who should be detested by critics. I wouldn't be doing my job if I was praised. It certainly polarised the critics but I think a lot of that was people who pretended to like *Trainspotting* because it was hip and being too scared to say that they hated it, then hating themselves and finally having the courage to say they detested *Filth*. Excellent. It's still early days for *Glue*, but in spite of, or because of, the great reviews, I don't expect it'll outsell *Filth*. They're different books: *Filth*'s a mad romp through a crazed character's head. *Glue*'s more considered, wider in its scope, but it doesn't necessarily make it a better book.

INT: What do you consider to be the key to a successful novel?

IW: The basic building blocks: good story, strong characters, honesty. I like novels set in a culture where the author comes from that culture and means it.

INT: It is a conscious move on your part to have certain places and characters reappear in your work.

IW: I can't be bothered inventing new characters who are the same as old ones. Also, you have to be responsible. I'm interested in subcultures – drugs, gadge, drink, football – and in a place the size of Leith, or even Edinburgh, not everybody is like that and the more characters you create like that, you start to unwittingly give that impression. Besides I'm interested. I want to know what happens to Rents or Sick Boy or what Bruce did in Australia. *Porno* is the *Trainspotting* crew ten years on. Because of that fact what the book is actually like will probably be lost. It'll be slagged off by the usual whingers (nothing I can do about that) and make loads of cash (nothing *they* can do about that). It's a romp, closer to *Filth* than *Glue*, but I'm very proud of it. Renton and Sick Boy and Spud and Begbie are no longer pals. It's racier than *Trainspotting* with more sex. Kind of 'Jackie Collins goes to Great Junction Street on a shopping trip and finds out that her credit cards have been stolen'.

INT: You have been writing for the stage, original screenplays and drama for television. How do these compare to the novel and the short story?

IW: I've worked on stage plays and screenplays. The whole thing is different, you're writing an enabling document, not the finished article. In screenwriting writers are generally treated like shit, when a screenplay is produced, everybody has a red pen, even people who have no creative input, like money men who get involved because movies are cool or they think that they'll get to fuck some actress.

They'd be better working in a bank. If a good film is made in Britain it's a happy accident. There are very few good writers working in film. Louis Mellis and David Scinto, the writers of *Sexy Beast*, are excellent. Peter Mullen and Paul Laverty are too. Most of the rest is clapped-out and formulaic shite. I only do it because you get the chance to work with people instead of being a lonely, sad bastard. I love the novel now. I used to slag it off but there are some great novels. I think they're getting better and will continue to do so. When you write a book you're like God so your ego can get out of control. That's why you need both, the humiliation game of screenwriting and the ego wanking of the novel.

INT: So, how then do you feel about your work when it is transferred to the big screen?

IW: A film of your novel has little to do with the book. It's a retelling of the story cinematically and there should be transformation. If anything I think adaptations suffer by trying to be too loyal to the book. I love the *Trainspotting* and *Acid House* films for different reasons, but I love them as films. But I always prefer the book to the film. Even in the case of *The Butcher Boy*: Neil Jordan's film was brilliant but it wasn't a patch on Patrick McCabe's book. We like to make our film of the book in our heads and we always end up in somebody else's head when we watch the picture.

INT: How do you see your work developing in the future?

IW: I can see myself becoming a genre writer. Sci-fi, crime, the historical romance, porn, the Western or Walter Scott style Highland romance. I'd like to pack it in and run a small bar in Greece or Thailand or the West Indies. Sink slowly into oblivion under a glorious sun. I won't do it, of course; I'm too hungry. My curse is I haven't written the book I want to yet.

Select criticism

■ Books

Craig, Cairns. *The Modern Scottish Novel: Narrative and National Imagination*. Edinburgh: Edinburgh University Press, 1999.

Redhead, Steve. *Repetitive Beat Generation*. Edinburgh: Rebel Inc., 2000.

■ Articles and chapters

Cardullo, Bert. 'Fiction into Film, or Bringing Welsh to a Boyle', *Literature Film Quarterly* 25: 3 (1997), pp. 158–62.

Freeman, Alan. 'Ghosts in Sunny Leith: Irvine Welsh's *Trainspotting*', in Susanne Hagemann, ed., *Studies in Scottish Fiction: 1945 to the Present*. Frankfurt: Peter Lang, 1996.

Gardiner, Michael. 'British Territory: Irvine Welsh in English and Japanese', *Textual Practice* 17: 1 (Spring 2003), pp. 101–17.

Herbrechter, Stefan. 'From *Trainspotting* to *Filth:* Masculinity and Cultural Politics in Irvine Welsh's Writings', in Russell West and Frank Lay, eds, *Subverting Masculinity: Hegemonic and Alternative Versions of Masculinity in Contemporary Culture*. Amsterdam: Rodopi, 2000.

Horton, Patricia. '*Trainspotting:* A Topography of the Masculine Abject', *English: The Journal of the English Association* 50: 198 (Autumn 2001), pp. 219–34.

Milne, Drew. 'The Fiction of James Kelman and Irvine Welsh: Accents, Speech and Writing', in Richard Lane, Rod Mengham and Philip Tew, eds, *Contemporary British Fiction*. Cambridge: Polity, 2003.

O'Hagan, Andrew. 'The Boys are Back in Town', in Ginette Vincendeau, ed., *Film/Literature/Heritage: A Sight and Sound Reader*. London: British Film Institute, 2001.

Paget, Derek. 'Speaking Out: The Transformations of *Trainspotting*', in Deborah Cartmell and Imelda Whelehan, eds, *Adaptations: From Text to Screen, Screen to Text*. London: Routledge, 1999.